Counting It Joy
The Macallister Story

Jody Macallister-Humbles

With contributions by
Bree (Macallister) Barela and Levi Macallister

FOR LEVI AND BREE

My precious children.
If no one else ever sees these pages,
may we remember the story
having rehearsed it together in real life.
Your dad gave me the best gifts for eternity:
You.

You have been brave, you have been noble, you have
been admirable. Our God is Faithful,
The Lifter of our heads.
Thank you for walking out our story in authenticity,
allowing it to be redeemed by Creator Lord
Who desires to bring freedom to all mankind
unto salvation and abundant life.
YOU are ACTIVE in His mission.
Good on ya!

I love you both – MADLY – forever.

CONTENTS

PROLOGUE

The reality is no place feels right when you've lost a spouse. No place feels like home. Whether you stay in the familiar, with close friends and community, or move on to the unfamiliar, someone is missing. And it feels odd to be surrounded by loved ones doing life, yet your beloved is not there. And it feels odd to be surrounded by new faces, attempting new life all the time wondering, *How did I get here?*

I suppose, - I hear, - at some point the new normal will prevail and home will be found again. I'm not there yet…

Mark moved to Heaven two and a half years ago. And it wasn't an easy move, as if any are. No, I don't believe anyone is ever truly ready to let a loved one go. But his was a move that, honestly, sometimes feels like defeat. It was by Mark's own hand after a battle that, in my finite vision, seemed insurmountable. It was one of those, *unless God steps in and intervenes…* He didn't. And though I can't make sense of it, I can trust God in it believing He loved Mark with a love beyond my comprehension. And because His ways are far above mine, because He makes all things work together for good for those who love Him, - I believe there is a story yet to be completed.

*****

I'm doing it, Mark. This is the book. Not the one you wanted me to write, nor the one I thought I would, but it seems the one God is prompting. To Him be the Glory.

In The Beginning

A FAIRY TALE

My first glimpse of Mark was through a church office window. As he rounded the corner and entered the training room, I already knew God was up to something. Isn't that bizarre? But I still see that moment, plain as day, and I still interpret it the same – God was up to something.

People have asked me over the years, would I do it all over again? Yes. I believe I would. How could I not? God stirred me at first sight of Mark and in two short weeks, He confirmed His active presence working in the both of us. I would do it again.

We were on our way to China. Mark, because God dropped a burden for Bible-less seekers in him. Me, because I had a heart for missions and I was attending a church active in *doing the stuff*. Mark was a fairly serious, self-proclaimed bachelor-to-the-rapture; I was in a relationship. Mark was a pastor from Albuquerque, NM; I had just graduated from college. Both of us had eyes set on ministry and the mission ahead, – something not quite the norm, – Bible smuggling.

It was July 1983 and China had just opened its doors – slightly – to tourism on an individual visa basis. After years of tight Communist control and little western access, the political tide changed and China was allowing small groups to enter its borders without the ever present tour guide and regulated agenda. Our little team of six was among the first from the free world to travel, on our own, throughout several of China's designated cities.

(Communist China still had its limits.)

What that meant was we paved our own way – for the good and the bad. For the good, we were not escorted through customs by Chinese officials thus allowing for safe(r) crossing of God's precious Word. We were able to set our own time table and not be ushered around to preset destinations. For the bad, Mark was assigned team leader (when all he wanted was to tag along). He had to manage the rest of us and the challenges that came our way.

And one of those challenges was me.

*****

Yes. There were six of us - a young married couple, three women (though I hardly considered myself one yet), and Mark. As soon as we hit Hong Kong, after just one night and day of training and some sightseeing, I came down sick. Because one of my roommates was a smoker and one had health issues requiring low air temperatures in our room as much as possible, even the common travel cold loomed large and appeared difficult to shake. Trip of a lifetime and I'm ill at day two with troubling thoughts of feverish days and missed exploits ahead. In tears, I presented Leader Mark my dilemma. And, voilá. In short order and with the approval of our Open Doors ministry authority, I moved in with Mark and became his roommate for the duration of our trip. (See what I mean about God being up to something? Really. What a set-up.)

So Mark became my *buddy* as our team was often paired up for activities, etc. Occasionally I partnered with the married gal, but rarely. She was pregnant and she and her husband paced themselves accordingly. The other two gals were older than me by a bit and seemed best in the company of one another. Reservations were made ahead of time for our Mainland China hotels - three rooms, two twin beds each - so Mark and I slid into all-things-companionship on about Day Three of our trip.

Hong Kong was incredible and I fell in love with the crowded, bustling city full of sky rises, trolleys, subways and ferries. I'm so not a city-lover so Hong Kong's attraction surprised me. Despite the burgeoning buildings and people, Hong Kong is beautiful with its bays and surrounding greenery, the ocean and the mountains. People from every corner of the globe add to its unique appeal. The real pull, however, was the ministry that took place there in Hong Kong. In an office building high above ground level, our little team was briefed for Bible couriering and we packed our suitcases to do our part in transporting life to Mainland China.

By God's grace six Americans, hearts varying in anxiety and excitement, passed through customs with our Bibles intact. I think perhaps my border crossing story was most unique in that I was questioned pretty thoroughly about the declaration of *loop earrings* on my customs form. This seemed to pique security interests and so distracted officials with the deliberation of what, exactly, *loop* meant that Mark and I were ultimately swished through customs as we were holding up the line. Mark always laughed when we rehashed our first border crossing.

We had several Bible deliveries to make to our Chinese contact and this involved some orchestration. We had to first connect with our contact and confirm that plans were still set for timing and location. With bugged, yes bugged, phone lines Mark had to set off for a neutral, preferably Chinese phone booth, to place a call and then had to navigate the English-Chinese language gaps. Then we had to hail cabs, stagger departures, and actually hope and pray it'd all come together on the other end. As I think back on it now, I remember Mark being very nervous when one of the gals and I were delayed in returning from our set rendezvous time. I'm not sure when Mark first started thinking, himself - God is up to something - but it may have been then. I remember how relieved he was to see me, but maybe he just felt responsible for me since I was his roommate and all.

Once our Bibles were gone, the rest of our trip was dedicated to sightseeing and some ministry research. Being on individual visas allowed for some exploration and Open Doors asked us to check out hotels as potential future lodging, and universities for English teaching opportunities. The time was ripe for believers to get inside China and do some damage!

Mark and I had a blast. We did most things with the team, of course, but when the young pregnant couple and the older ladies were taking things slow, Mark and I hopped on bikes and went exploring. And in China 1983 this was no small adventure. We got lost and all turned around more than once, but since we were trained to keep a *go with the flow* mindset, every wrong turn seemed ordained and the life we were able to see off the beaten paths was often both exhilarating and sobering.

God began to knead my heart for China and her people, and Mark was interconnected with my shaping. One Sunday morning, the six of us headed to the Communist-approved, Three Self Church. I don't know what I expected and I knew it wasn't free, rather government controlled, yet I cried hearing familiar hymns sung by Chinese believers following Jesus the best they knew how. One song, "On Christ the Solid Rock I Stand," I remembered singing with my great grandma as a little girl and it just about wrecked me. I remember Mark looking at me and getting all misty-eyed himself and he told me lots later that it was a revealing moment for him, seeing me so touched by Jesus and God's people in worship.

By this time, I knew Mark was part of my China package. I still didn't know what God was up to - exactly - but I knew it was important. I realized I really didn't know much about Mark, though we began sharing our stories some. We didn't have a lot of time in the evenings – so full were our days, but we did have a little before the lights went off each night.

Towards the end of our trip, we had a big evening at Tiananmen Square - mingling, Frisbee playing, kite flying and talking with countless young Chinese interested in speaking English. God had an amazing gift for us, too: a hoped-for connection with a Chinese *underground* believer. As a team, we'd all prayed for the opportunity to meet a Christian but knew that would only come about by God's sovereignty; those guys don't wear placards. Because it was dangerous to be caught openly speaking *Jesus*, Mark and I peeled off from the team and the crowd we'd gathered and wandered down a small side street with our new found brother, Jeff. Mark had been carrying a small New Testament for such a time as this and was overjoyed at being able to present it to this young man who was eager to receive it, yet was risking his freedom to take it. Another exhilarating and sobering moment.

It was late by the time we managed to get back to Tiananmen. For safety's sake we had to wander awhile and then say farewell to Jeff, mid route, so as not to return together. I know it sounds crazy, but watchful eyes were everywhere. China was just opening her doors and foreigners were suspect though welcomed for the sake of China's front to the free world. By the time Mark and I got back to the Square, our team members had returned to the hotel so we promptly hailed a cab and jumped in the back seat. Then I, just as promptly, laid my head down on Mark's lap and he - equally promptly - leaned down and kissed my forehead.

*****

I wish I could remember that next morning more clearly.

What I do recall is packing up and gathering with the team for one more meal in Mainland China before our plane was to take us back to Hong Kong. We had just one more night in Asia before we'd be heading home. And my heart was a bit of a mess. I'd fallen in love with China, and I'd fallen in love with Mark - though I don't think I was clearheaded enough to admit that yet.

I remember a friend of mine saying, long ago, - God tricks us into relationships and marriage. We'd laugh at that and yet, though I wouldn't word it quite that way, I see some truth to the idea. What happened on our way out of China was a clincher to the ponder, *God, what are You up to?*

Our little team of six arrives at the Beijing airport where we soon discover the plane was vastly overbooked. Only in China. There were some important looking men from India who apparently wanted to take that flight and apparently were getting the preferential treatment. No amount of pleading on Mark's part (he was team leader, remember) could convince the gate attendant that we six Americans needed to get back to Hong Kong to catch our international flight on time. Didn't matter. What was crazier still? Slow motion became fast and there was one seat left on the plane. Mark told me to board. - What I learned in the slow mo time frame was that there was not another Hong Kong bound flight leaving Beijing that day. What I learned later was Mark had to route the young couple to another city to catch a flight out of Mainland. He stayed back with the ladies and arranged for a red-eye, or close to it, to connect with the Hong Kong - LAX flight the next morning.

So I get on the plane and my mind is racing. Mark kissed me last night, this morning was a blur, and now I'm on a plane by myself back to Hong Kong - did I say *by myself?* We were supposed to be flying back to Hong Kong together and doing a little debriefing with the Open Doors base there before heading home the next morning. I was supposed to have my roommate one more night.

As plane engines revved for take-off, I wasn't sure I'd even see my team members again this side of the ocean. Who knew when they'd really be able to get out of China? (I'd heard stories.) Though my *go with the flow* attitude didn't fail me, I still felt disappointed at the turn of events. We didn't get a chance to say goodbye or compile our notes, or…

I was pondering these things as the plane raced down the runway and lifted off. Simultaneously there was a large clanking noise that got the attention of the passengers. An English speaking, mechanical engineer seated next to me twisted forward and back trying to see what was going on outside the plane and said, under breath, "That didn't sound right," when the air masks dropped from the overhead compartments. And not all of them dropped. Just a scattered few here and there. And then I thought I knew why only one of us boarded that plane.

I can laugh about it now, but in the moment I was fairly convinced that plane was gonna crash and it would be just too heartbreaking for a team of six Americans to perish in a land far away. Nope, only one would die and that would be me.

I began to pray and I know others around me were seeing their lives flash before their eyes while processing our scenario. It was a quiet, sober bunch waiting for some word from our pilot. When that came, we were told we'd be landing within 20 minutes. And we did, safely - Praise God - and sat in a tiny, little airport in the middle of nowhere while the plane's engine was worked on for over two hours. Then, zoom - right back in to the air again Hong Kong bound.

I was so thankful, I was bursting. I wasn't sure what was going on back in China with my teammates, but I was alive and fully ready for the adventure ahead of me, no matter what that was to look like.

*****

I landed in Hong Kong and went straight to the Airport Hotel which felt like home to me now compared to the Third World lodging we had in China. The Mainland in 1983 was considered to be, at least, 20 years behind the most average of America's cities. I would say that was an optimistic consensus. In any case, I loved the HK Airport Hotel and its restaurants and modern gleam from the first night we stayed there prior to our China stint. I checked in to my room and immediately called Open Doors to report the lot of my teammates and to see if I could be of service by debriefing, myself, with one of the leaders. Fortunately I was able to do that over the phone; I was ready to relax and wasn't overly anxious to travel the city on my own.

And I took a bubble bath.

Funny how I remember that. Here I was in this beautiful hotel, by myself, in a mysterious famed city, in a magnificent bathtub and I felt this incredible draw to the place. It was quiet, all alone there, and God began wooing my heart for Asia.

And even more so for Hong Kong. I loved what it represented: a gateway to numerous countries, a training ground to reach access-restricted Asia and the persecuted church. In this highly modern city, God was doing a work that served His suffering bride in every direction. Christians from all over the western world came here to be equipped to reach family behind the Bamboo Curtain. A seed was planted in me and I wanted to be a part of that work.

*****

I might have been clean and jammied up for an hour when the phone rang. It was Mark calling from the Mainland. "Jody, I miss you. I realized when you got on that plane without me that I wasn't ready to say goodbye. Would you consider extending your trip and stopping in Hawaii with me for a few days on our way home?"

Just like that. Wow.

*****

Whether we traveled part way home as a team, or not, I can't remember now, but I remember deplaning in Honolulu and thinking I was living a fairy tale. - Mark and I found a hotel right on the beach and since we'd already been roommates for over two weeks, it seemed perfectly natural to continue doing so now. We spent three or four wonderful days and nights roaming the island and on the beach. One evening we visited a Calvary Chapel and worshiped in a small, intimate setting with a group of welcoming believers. It was the first time I'd heard Mark sing and I remember thinking he had a nice voice. Another night we had dinner at a Bobby McGee's (Mark's pick) and I had a Mai Tai that made Mark smile and laugh at me a lot.

We talked. And talked. And talked some more. And honestly, this was kind of new for me. I wasn't a huge talker. But Mark was and apparently he wanted to know everything about me there was to know. Imagine.

All too soon it was time to return to real life, - Mark to Albuquerque and me to So Cal, back to work and the things we'd left behind.

*****

For the most part, I'm not one who wants to go back and relive life and redo its seasons. But every once in a while, I'd like to go visit my fairy tale. - And I have, many times in my mind, in the tough seasons. I've reminded myself that divine circumstances brought Mark and me together; no one but God could have written such a magical script. Even now as I put to paper our history, I'm awed by the beauty of that 1983 trip to China, and I'm thankful - despite everything - that God "tricked" me into life with Mark.

*****

Was it that night after we said quick airport goodbyes or the next day that Mark called and our distance-dating began? It wasn't long, I know that. Mark had some explaining to do back in New Mexico as to his delayed return; I had some on my end as well. But it took, and before long, Mark flew me out to Albuquerque to further establish and evaluate our relationship. Funny. We weren't roommates this trip. I stayed at Mark's little cabin in the mountains and he stayed in town with friends. I can still see the comforter on his bed and loved being all wrapped up in it one night while experiencing my first New Mexico thunderstorm. It was a little intimidating, but a treat nonetheless.

At church the Sunday of my visit, Pastor Skip gave a message entitled "It Just so Happened" all about God's sovereignty in the life of Moses and applied to our lives today. Do you think that wasn't solidifying in my life at the moment? Oh my gosh. It just so happened that Mark and I were on the same China team out of all the countless ones we could have been on separately. It just so happened that God allowed me to become ill in Hong Kong and our team was constructed in such a manner that Mark and I became roommates. It just so happened that we experienced, together, opportunities in China that ravished our hearts. It just so happened that we had fun together and had any attraction at all to one another. It just so happened that I boarded a plane and Mark stayed behind. It just so happened we took our chances and made Hawaii work. It just so happened.

It's good for me to remember...

*****

Back home again, I dove in to all things China. My church was engaging, full-speed ahead, with Open Doors Asia and was asked to be its training base for anyone wanting to go to China from North America. Now that Mainland had opened its doors, there was a flood of interested believers raring to go, thus we were busy in Lancaster. I was involved with teams and support-raising and administration, and Mark was restless back in Albuquerque away from the action and from me. For the time being, as much as I missed him and missed doing this deal with him, it was a sweet time of long letters and phone conversations. In many ways, I feel it was our most intimate season of getting to know one another without the encumbrances of the "dance" of presence.

One thing that also solidified our relationship was a choice I had to make. Because of the unique experience of being in Hong Kong alone one night when God spoke to me about ministry there, and because I took that to another level and talked about it with the Hong Kong staff, - I was invited to move there and become a part of the base team. Heart pulling. The choice: Mark or Hong Kong. Not both. Not then anyway. - Mark was ready to move to California to pursue me and the China ministry, but he made it clear that if I chose Hong Kong, he was making no promises to be there when my season was over. - When looking to my pastor, Brent, for wisdom, he asked me the question, "What do you want to do?" and freed me from over thinking. I chose Mark, though I'll say it wasn't all easy. (Hong Kong still pulls me to this day.)

Mark moved to the desert by the end of the year and we continued growing in like mindedness and love. On my birthday, April 1st, Mark took me to Lake Arrowhead to celebrate and to ask me to marry him.

The next day he played Indian Giver and took back his proposal - the first recognizable sign of trouble.

SETTING THE STAGE

I remember driving home just baffled by Mark's cold feet. From Day One God seemed to be directing our relationship. I mean it did "just so happen" and I didn't see any yellow flags, let alone red ones, on the horizon. Our friendship and dating were pretty smooth sailing (not without any challenges, but nothing out of the ordinary when two people begin binding their lives together). Crushed was maybe a better word than baffled.

And Mark offered very little explanation. At least not immediately. We drove home in silent misery. After such a high the night before: a beautiful drive up the mountains, a dinner out in the lovely village of Lake Arrowhead, and a camp-out of sorts in a little rustic cabin, - every recollection went south with Mark's, "Sorry Jody, I can't marry you after all."

We pulled into my driveway and went inside quietly. I was still living at my family home at the time and I'm sure anyone who witnessed our arrival was thinking, "uh oh." I'm not sure if Mark was ready to talk or not, but I needed some assurance that the whole marriage conversation wasn't a dead-end. Back to baffled...

We went to my room and the story began to unravel.

"I had a nervous breakdown, Jody." - And my heart ached right there for the pain and burden he carried somehow believing it dampened any hope for joy and relationship in his future. He was afraid. He was fearful to marry and involve another person in his plight, even though in this season, he was fine and didn't know what his future held. How could he?

Mark had been 20ish and the perfect storm surrounded his life when he was first hospitalized, - some crazy family genetics (depression, epilepsy, alcoholism, a brain tumor, grand and petty mal seizures), a broken home, negligent biological parents and dysfunctional step parents to name the foundation. He'd been prescribed and taken some nasty, hardcore medication to stave off borderline errant brain waves in his own head. To make matters worse, perhaps, Mark had recently committed his life to Jesus when the bottom hit. So the spiritual dynamic, being a baby believer, guilted him into self-condemnation and a real loneliness about his life and circumstances.

All this Mark confessed to me spilling out things I imagined he'd never shared with anyone before, - except for maybe a counselor or two during his quest for sanity. I asked questions and he answered them with as much honesty and clarity as he possessed at the time and as we processed his story, we came to the conclusion that it was his past. Yes, he'd broken but look how far he'd come. He was strong and healthy, had forgiven the perpetrating family members, was no longer on meds, and was a pastor, for crying out loud. Surely he was a new man.

So the wedding date was set: July 21, 1984. Exactly one year following our return date from Hawaii.

*****

Somewhere around this same time, Mark was asked to come on board the local church staff and oversee the China ministry. I had been working as Pastor Brent's secretary/church receptionist for a few months and life just couldn't get any better. It seemed the fairy tale had a stateside sequel and we were living it. Mark was in the office, fully engaged, in orchestrating training and trip planning for teams that would come through our little Southern California base before heading overseas to China. I served more the church as a whole, but was right alongside on weekends as we traveled up the local mountains to a lovely ranch location where the hosting/ training took place. There were things going on all week also:

Chinese dinners for fundraising, prayer meetings, newspaper bundling. (What's that about? Well . . . Part of the trip travel costs for those participating from our home church were paid for by the community effort of newspaper recycling. I have a lot of fun memories of spending Saturdays driving all over the Valley and picking up discarded newspapers; now folks are legitimately employed providing that service.)

So you get the idea. Our lives were consumed with China focus. And it wasn't just Mark's and mine, though we may have been near the top of the list. The entire church was diligently committed to getting God's Word into the hands of Chinese believers, that His name would be glorified and evangelism and discipleship furthered. Those were exciting days.

Mark and I, as part of our marriage preparation, went through some pre-marital counseling. It was good. I remember hammering out issues and areas of present/potential conflict. I remember being absolutely enamored with the idea of submission to Mark. He was to be the head of our household, anointed for the role by the Living God of the Universe. Where was there a safer, more secure, place on earth to be than in submission to one's husband? I remember some pretty candid confessions about many shortcomings, values, and *stupid thinking*, - but I don't remember talking about Mark's past when it came to his breakdown. That was over and behind him - not to touch us in the future. Not worth discussing. Though we set a wedding date before the conclusion of our counseling, we received the blessing of our authorities and from proposal to culmination there were three and a half months.

Whew.

THE WEDDING & THE HONEYMOON (PT. I & II)

The most wonderful, beautiful ever. Is that what every bride says?

I loved my wedding. That beautiful ranch, where all the China training took place, was the site of the first-ever-to-be-held-there wedding. Thanks to my mom and several friends the day was glorious. I was never much of an event planner, so besides giving my mom colors, I think she did everything else. I mean I tried on a wedding dress, but she made me - ha - so indifferent was I to the details. I'm tempted to insert a color photo of my cake here; it was perfect. So simple and awesome. Teal. Green teal and silver. Gorgeous on the Ranch lawn.

Friends routed directions along the roadside between Lancaster and Three Points so the out-of-towners could find their way. Some folks painted the grape arbor trellis; others hauled chairs and tables from town and set them all up for ceremony and reception. Another special friend created an awesome buffet luncheon. - I'm sure there were all kinds of things going on behind the scenes that I never knew about, but I wish I did. I'd like to say, "Thanks again," even now.

How many thoughts swim through a person's mind as he or she, the groom or bride, is trying to sleep the night before the wedding day? Countless, countless thoughts. All excited and hopeful for a future of love and sharing and growing together. My mind swam with the certainty, due to our fairy tale meeting, that Mark and I were headed for an adventuresome future. Little did I know.

17

*****

As I was readying to walk down the aisle with my dad and bridesmaids, Mark was wandering around the ranch grounds, in his red shorts, talking with everyone arriving for our special event. I can see it happening plain as day. So many people told me afterwards they were getting a kick out of him just visiting so casually and enjoying the reunions. He was all joy and happiness and in no hurry to cut short any hug or joke or conversation. I love envisioning Mark so carefree; it's a cherished memory. Finally, enough folks told him he'd better be thinking about getting dressed. And a wedding commenced.

Mark and I were married by two men: a hero of mine, Brent Rue, and a hero of Mark's, Skip Heitzig. And there was rich meaning in that combination - one that would take on even more meaning as the years went by. And some that would manifest within a few short weeks.

There was laughter and fun and a horse drawn carriage. After the ceremony was complete, the cake applied properly to mouths as is the custom, an exit was made by another ranch "first" - a bowlered hat driver escorting Mark and me off the property by horse and buggy. So sweet. - And then it was a tag team from one vehicle to another all the way back to Lake Arrowhead for Part I of our honeymoon. - Probably because I had so little to do with pulling off my wedding, I wasn't as exhausted as many a bride after her big day, - but I do remember falling asleep while soaking in a bubble bath before a late night dinner. Guess it's inherent in bride definition: tired. There was no camping out this go-round. Mark chose the beautiful Arrowhead Resort and though we were there less than 24 hours, it still was a refreshing and healing stay after the previous one. No doubt, eh?

By noon the next day, we were dashing to LAX for Honeymoon Part II in Hawaii. We had to return there also and enjoy the warm Pacific waters as Mr and Mrs Macallister. The consensus today is Oahu is no place to vacation, - too crowded, commercial, etc. But we didn't mind then. With no time constraints and no schedules, Mark and I roamed the Island and did everything there was to do. My favorite was just water rafting and lounging at the beach. There's something magical about lying in the ocean and not being cold. I know Mark liked that also, - that and Waimea Bay hangs. Relaxing.

We rested so much we missed our flight to Hong Kong. Well it wasn't a rest issue, but a *what the heck time zone do we apply to our ticket?* We showed up at the airport - right on time - but a day late. Geez. I think our tickets were purchased thru China Air and all dates were China's, a little confusing as you pass the International Date Line going west. Ah well. The ticket agents smiled patronizingly and got us on a flight Hong Kong bound without problem; fortunate for us.

THE HONEYMOON (PT. III)

Everyone told us we were crazy to head to China for our honeymoon. Nothing romantic about that, yet it was our story. We were retracing steps.

And I loved Hong Kong, remember. - The Open Doors staff gifted us two nights at the gorgeous Harbor View Hotel. Now that was amazing. Unbelievable view of Hong Kong's skyline and waters, Five Star rooms and exercise/spa facilities, shops, restaurants, etc. Loved that place. - So much of our stay in Hong Kong was pure honeymoon, though we did spend time with friends and Open Doors staff preparing for yet another trip into the Mainland. All good.

Though China was a different story, it was still incredibly special traveling with Mark again to places that tugged on our hearts, whether because of sweet memories made the previous year or because God was showing us His loves and His heartaches. Both aspects were evident.

We made it safely across the border, yet again, and dispensed with our Bibles as soon as possible. So from there on out it was more research for the ministry and if one pays attention, anything can be educational. Mark and I took an overnight train ride between Shanghai and Beijing where we bunked up with two 20 something Chinese young men in a four bunk, tiny berth. I think Mark was concerned with how I was processing that one, but anything cross cultural in those days was exciting to me. The men were fun, funny and very inquisitive as to why a newly married couple would be riding a train in China.

They shared their own stories and we had reason to be a little sad in parting, such fun had we visiting, eating and sleeping together!

Though we spent time in the same places as our 1983 trip, we also incorporated another city. Hangzhou, famous for its beauty and gorgeous full moon settings. It was quite nice, though Mark got sick and missed much of it. Would you believe I ventured out on my own some, though it wasn't nearly as fun? It wasn't without company, though. In 1983 and 84, young people still flocked to westerners to practice their English speaking attempts. And a stray western female got plenty of attention. I have some photos taken with a couple young men who kept me thinking with their questions - mostly about idioms and *how you say?*

Not "nearly as fun" should actually be preceded with, "I didn't want to leave Mark," but he was always one to push me beyond me. Whether in the big things or the small things, Mark never let my apprehension stop him from encouraging me to do something. I didn't always appreciate those exhortations, but in hindsight I've stretched more than I ever would have without him. - I didn't see any of that then, I was just bummed that he was sick and I was doing China without him.

*****

At least our exit from China went smoother than our first one. We left hopeful that God had plans for us in Asia, somewhere, somehow. We were hooked, burdened by the plight of our family behind the Bamboo Curtain and drawn to the ministry that allowed us - in some small way -to be bearers of Good News to them.

And our trip wasn't quite over. We had a little more time to wander Hong Kong and be a part of some great things that were happening there. In 1984, Great Britain still claimed Hong Kong as one of her colonies though there was already talk of China's takeover in the following decade. - But for now Hong Kong was free and how glorious it was to see God's hand active in so many ministries. Mark and I had the privilege of meeting Jackie Pullinger and staying at her camp where she (and her co-laborers) literally prayed young drug-addicted men off the streets and out of their addictions. We participated in an international conference, connected with other ministries doing great works in the mainland, and just took it all in so as to be better equipped for this overseas venture.

Before heading home, we finished our Asia trip about 30 minutes, by ferry, outside Hong Kong on Lama Island. A couple who trained teachers for China's university campuses, - still one of the best options for missions in countries where missions are not allowed – had a beachfront condo there. We had a decent little room to ourselves complete with geckos on the walls - live ones. So tropical was the island and so beyond the fast-paced, city life of Hong Kong that all sorts of live critters felt totally comfortable entering any doorway or window they desired. It was a little unnerving waking up to reptiles near my body, but, hey - whatcha gonna do?

Also before heading home, Mark and I fought. And it was crazy and I still think it's crazy. And many times over the years, I've thought about that argument and the significance of it. Not that we didn't make up, forgive one another and move on. We did. But it was strange and senseless. I know that's true of most arguments people have; there's misinterpretation and escalation and either woundedness or anger or both. - I was just rather stunned. Really? Now? About this? - Not quite the note I wanted to end our honeymoon on, but I chalked it up to life. The good and the bad; we get both.

HOME AGAIN & BACK & FORTH

There were wedding presents to open and details - like getting into a place of our own - to figure out once we got stateside again. Not sure what we were thinking, but we stayed with my parents for a little bit until a cute little one bedroom apartment opened up and we moved in as most newlyweds do: with few belongings and lots of zeal for the future. We were still full-fledged involved with church and the China ministry in the same way as previous to our wedding. Lots of administrative orchestrating, training of Bible couriers, prayer meetings, international communicating, etc. It was a very exciting season. Between 1983 and late 1985, Mark and I made five trips to Asia. There was a big effort to blitz China with Bibles as the time was ripe to do so, - a little less scrutiny of tourists and lots more of them due to the incorporating of individual travel visas. People from all over the world were flooding China's gates and, we Christians wanted to flow in on that flood, less obtrusive, incognito in the masses. Mark spearheaded the Open Doors' North American participation and was either leading teams or needing to be overseas to help out on that end of things.

I wish I could recall all the scenarios of those trips. I remember some interesting things like when, - on one team's border crossing we all made it safely through, only to be suspiciously followed and photographed at our hotel restaurant. We prayed like crazy for the safety of our Chinese counterparts - always - as they were definitely more at risk than we westerners ever were. That's why getting through the border was never our biggest concern. No. The lives of our believing family, the recipients of God's precious Word, were who we constantly considered in our efforts and actions.

Another time Mark and a friend did get caught at the border. It was a bit intimidating and that's exactly what the Chinese officials aimed for. They took the two guys into a little room and interrogated them loudly, taking away their Bibles and warning them to never try that again. Our team had to split up and travel separately in waiting taxis and shuttles, finding our way individually to our hotel, staggering our arrival so as not to appear connected in any way. That would have been disastrous to our intentions if any of us would have been linked to those lawbreakers.

(Once, a beloved Hong Kong Chinese friend and counterpart was caught at one of Mainland's borders. It was pretty bad. Our friend was detained for 72 hours, if I remember right, and it did something to him. I don't know the details as he was never able to express them, but I think whatever was done to him was humiliating and awful. Or maybe he broke and revealed some things that none of us ever wanted spoken to Chinese authorities. [He wouldn't have been the first and our hearts would have instantly forgiven him.] He was a mess for a long time and the weight of what we were about hit heavy. - Westerners, especially Americans and Europeans, could avoid significant problems when caught at the border - such a political game - because China wanted to present a *face* to the free world of openness and accommodation. Hong Kong Chinese (though still *free* at the time) messed with China's authority a little too close to home. --- So imagine the consequences to discovered believers inside the country. Frightening. Wrong.)

On a lighter note, there were some pretty funny jet lag stories. When our teams would arrive in Hong Kong it would usually be fairly early in the day. We'd have to stay awake for hours to adapt to the time zone and that was easier for some than others. I remember folks sitting down for a midday meal, cocking their heads to one side and being instantly asleep. One time there were about eight of us walking to lunch and one guy fell asleep midstride. Another guy had to grab him as he was veering into oncoming pedestrians.

Peking Duck and family meals. - Most of our Mainland eating was in typical family style. Years ago, all the restaurants had big round tables that would seat ten to twelve people and that's how we ate, day in, day out, in China. It was wonderful, actually. We westerners could learn a thing or two about the beauty of friends and family dining from the Asians... And everyone always had to try out Peking Duck while in Peking. I mean, really.

Strange things happened, too. Creepy things. On sightseeing one day in Mainland China our team visited a temple area of sorts with mini shrines all over and food offerings being made to appease and feed the dead along their way to wherever they were going. That was crazy enough, but stranger still, was a monument at the temple center crawling with cats. Live scrawny cats were all over that thing. As I looked towards it, one cat caught my eye and I swear I was looking straight at a demonic being. I got lots of prayer after that. Though I strongly believed greater was He in me, than he (my adversary) in the world, I still didn't know what attempts the enemy might make to mess with me after that experience. Me or Mark.

Another time Mark and I were in the Philippines at a beautiful mountain resort in Baguio. We had the privilege of attending an Open Doors Asia conference and were so excited to be there. The hotel was spectacular, very south-pacific-tropical feeling. The fellowship was awesome; the Holy Spirit showed up; the food was great. However. Something crazy demonic happened in the night. . . Mark and I were sound asleep when suddenly I was jolted awake and I knew Mark was also awakened lying rigidly beside me. Neither of us moved, but we whispered our awareness of a darker-than-night darkness in the room. The oppression was thick and heavy nailing us to the bed. We prayed. We called on the name of Jesus. We were finally able to turn on a light and dispel some of the darkness, but it was a battle all night long. What was that about? Being in an enemy stronghold in the high places of the Philippines? Enraging our adversary with the plans and purposes of Open Doors' conference? Nighttime vulnerability and an attempt to be thwarted and intimidated by demonic powers? - I don't know, but it was scary. Mark and I got prayer the next day, but I still wasn't excited about turning off the light that night and going to sleep. Though it wasn't an incredibly restful night, still it wasn't horrific like the night before. - Ultimately, I was awakened to the truth of the very real spiritual battle we were in.

*****

So. Why include these stories? To remember that Mark's life and my life were more than the sum of his illness. Because there were times when nothing seemed extractable from the glaring challenge of Mark's reality, times when it seemed that was all life was about.

*****

Sometime along the way of our back and forth trips across the ocean, Mark and I decided to move overseas. It was a logical progression of our Asia involvement, but also my love and excitement of Hong Kong grabbed Mark also. He was previously more interested in moving to mainland China but came to believe he was more useful in a "training of others" capacity and Hong Kong was perfect for that. What we'd done in California for North America, we could do in Hong Kong for the world.

One tiny event stands out in the many of our travels when I consider pinpoints of Mark's health. We were visiting a good friend from California who was teaching English as a second language in Mainland China. It was so great to see him, wander his university and do a little sightseeing with him and his girlfriend one day. At some point we had them return to our hotel room where we did our favorite thing: talk about China and plan and strategize for future ministry there. While we were talking, Mark crossed the room, laid down on the bed and went fast asleep. And he slept for a long while. I remember being a slight bit irritated that he'd do that while we had guests. I was also somewhat concerned he might be coming down with something (he'd been sick before in China, remember). I think he rallied some prior to our friends leaving for the night, but he was pretty sluggish. No, he didn't feel sick. He wasn't sure what was going on.

No further incidences on that trip. And once we got home, we began to prepare for our move to Hong Kong. We had the blessing of our church, the surrender of our parents, the enthusiasm of our friends. Though I became more nervous as the timetable was set in motion, I was excited about living in a foreign country and finally becoming the missionary - of sorts - that I'd always dreamed of. The nerves came into play, because Mark was not feeling great. I don't remember how that manifest, exactly, but I think most noticeable were his sleep habits or lack thereof. - Mark never was a consistent, good sleeper, but I wasn't too concerned initially. He seemed to manage okay and actually had way more energy than me and most people I knew.

Somewhere in our departure preparations, Mark expressed experiencing some anxiety also. I think I chalked that up to international move jitters, although I was concerned. I could see he was struggling, but he didn't verbalize it much and kept pushing forward. (In hindsight, I think he was fighting fear about what was happening, - maybe thinking he could beat the beast if he didn't give in.)

One thing Mark wanted to do before leaving the States was to visit our family members who lived outside of California. Once we left the continent, who knew how long it'd be before we'd be back to see any of them again? So once we packed up our little apartment and put all our life's possessions into a storage unit, we began the rounds of family visits. Though Mark hadn't slept in two or three days, we hopped on a plane and headed to Oregon, kind of a *come hell or high water* decision in retrospect.

*****

Mark's brother, Mike, fetched us from the airport and we headed to the Oregon Mac home: first stop. - It's funny how some memories are so vivid and others are completely gone, but I clearly see Mark and me standing in the guest bedroom perplexed about the escalation of his anxiety. We knew he needed to sleep - badly - by this time. Now that we were on our way and beyond the pack up, etc, I was hopeful Mark could let-down and rest.

He didn't. He couldn't.

And it wasn't long until the anxiety was unbearable and we were headed to the hospital. Mark's worst fear and my unbelief. I remember a doctor's description of "anxiety" at this juncture, - like cigarettes being put out all over your skin. Mark felt that. God. How could it be this bad?

HOSPITAL #1

Much of this hospitalization is a blur to me, except that I remember what the rooms looked like and how it felt to walk into Mark's as he was hallucinating. It was the drugs, I was assured, combined with the sleeplessness. It would just take a few days to bring him around. It was horrible. Fortunately, the hallucinations themselves weren't horrible, just the fact that he was having them. Mark saw his childhood kitty, Toedy, in the corner of his room and it seemed to bring him joy. He talked to him quite a bit. It scared me.

I didn't really know Mark's brother and his wife well at this stage of our lives. This trip was meant to change that. But under the circumstances, and as I was needing some real God-family support, I went and stayed with a couple who lived not far from the hospital and who were previously from our church in California. This was the grace I needed as I borrowed their car and traveled back and forth from the hospital for about 10 days. Slowly, slowly Mark came around with some heavy duty medications and managed to sleep with their help. I was relieved; he was relieved. But the more he turned around, the more aware he became that he just had another nervous breakdown and that was not good.

*****

Needless to say, our Hong Kong plans were on indefinite hold. And our little around-the-States trip came to a screeching halt, also. Mark and I stayed in Oregon for a few more days after his hospital discharge to give him more rest and some semblance of normalcy before hopping back on a plane and returning to California to an uncertain future. Our friends were gracious and so hospitable caring for us, praying over us and allowing us space to process what just happened with minimal questions or dialogue. They simply provided an environment of love and acceptance - just what we needed. I felt bad for Mark's brother and sister-in-law whom we came to see as we didn't go back to their house, but they were gracious also and seemed to understand our need for spiritual/familiar family at the time.

Mark and I returned to California and went to my parents' home; I'm sure that was hard for Mark. I know he hated his vulnerability and dependency. It was bad enough that he broke again and was hospitalized, but worse because he wasn't really well now either. We'd given up our jobs since we were Hong Kong bound and life seemed in limbo for the time being.

I hadn't a clue what to expect of Mark at this juncture; I'd never been through anything like this before. I learned quickly, though, that mental breakdowns take a huge toll on every fiber of a person's being. The weariness that finally overtakes and overcomes the fight against it doesn't go away quickly. Mark was exhausted. For every iota of anxiety he'd previously experienced there was now an equal measure in depression. The meds had tackled the sleeplessness, but now Mark couldn't wake up.

I think by this stage, we were about four months into this monstrous season, far enough along to where I started raking my memory for clues and indicators of how it all began. I think my first flag was that "inappropriate" nap taken in China. From there it was a blitz of activity and some workaholic tendencies Mark demonstrated keeping him awake all hours of the night, only to continue for days on end. And now several months into depression I, admittedly, became frustrated and sometimes short on patience myself. I wanted Mark to get up out of that bed and do something. My mind would scream those words. I thought if he'd get focused and busy, we could get back on track with our lives. We'd had a bump in the road but it didn't need to totally derail us.

About the only activity Mark and I experienced in those days was that which incorporated our pursuit of his wellness. We tried everything. We saw endocrinologists and chemical biologists. We drove hours to get prayer from those who were gifted in spiritual warfare. Mark engaged in some counseling, though half-heartedly. (He'd been there before and didn't see any point in rehashing his family and upbringing components.) We tried nutritionists and treated for hypoglycemia and other mood altering illnesses. He did a sleep study and attempted therapeutic exercise programs. And the list goes on.

I was frustrated but I was also very optimistic, naively so. I look back now and think I really didn't get it. Not that God couldn't have met my optimism and trumped it with the miraculous, but I didn't understand the depths of Mark's valley. Day after day after day he would lay in bed alternately sleeping then awake with eyes open staring at the ceiling. I would sit with him and talk to him and encourage (exhort) him to do *something* all to no avail. He was stuck.

*****

Before I was married, I prayed a dangerous prayer: God, cause me to marry someone who will lead me closer to you. - I really loved my Savior and truly wanted to know Him in a deep and enduring way. I wanted my husband, whoever that might be, to enhance that desire. But, you've heard it before: be careful what you ask for. Sometimes I think I was just plain stupid to pray that prayer. Seriously God? You know what I meant. I didn't mean this. I didn't want to be drawn closer to You through pain and anxiety and fear.

But...

In my frustration and growing despair in the natural, in the spiritual, God began to meet me. As much as I wanted to be there for Mark, I could not sit in that house one more day and just wait while Mark slept or lay there listless. I packed up my Bible and a notebook and headed to the local college library where I spent my own *day after day* in God's company pouring over the story of Moses and God's deliverance of His people. Day after day, I cried out, "Let Mark go," such as Moses cried out "Let my people go." I read all the commentary; I filled pages galore of notes and what God was revealing to me through our time together. And I treasured those many hours. I was amazed how God showed up for me every time I sat with Him. I was filled with a fresh awareness of His love for me and His love for Mark. My optimism became more grounded in faith and a belief that God had a deliverance ahead for the Macallisters.

It was still hard to return to Mark's side after my library visits - like coming off the mountain - so much did I want Mark to share my hope and vision. I agonized at his indifference, his disinterest. However, that same hope went a long ways and, in those days, I was able to encourage more and exhort less.

Funny thing though, or, not so funny. Mark didn't get better, he got worse. As weeks went by, Mark began to get angry. At me, primarily. I didn't get it. I mean, yeah who else could he get mad at? I was the only person he ever saw. But I was only ever thinking of him and caring for him and trying to help him get better. I had all kinds of theories as to what this was about - from, he's mad because I'm well and he's not, to: he just needs to yell at someone and get it out. Again, - I was very new at this stuff, but I tried to be patient and kind and thought I was doing a decent job of it.

At some point, Mark was done with it all - but not in a good way. I vividly remember him getting out of bed, getting dressed, taking the car keys and flying out the front door. He said he couldn't take it anymore and was leaving, - I wouldn't see him again because his life was over. I was crying and begging him not to leave and we made a bit of a scene outside at the car if anyone was around to see us. I held on to him, but he was gruff enough to push me away and off he went. I was devastated. What did this mean? Would he take his life? Would I ever hear his voice again? Where was the deliverance I thought God was bringing? Was this where my hope was betrayed?

Mark and I had a friend and coworker at our church office who was formerly a policeman or maybe a state sheriff. I didn't know what to do so I called him and told him what was going on. I had no details, no clues as to which direction Mark might go, but our friend told me he'd put out some notices for the police to be on the lookout for a little beige Kharmann Ghia. And then I waited.

*****

I have two sisters who lived in Santa Barbara at the time - one at Westmont College, the other holding down a job there in the city. Throughout Mark's and my ordeal, my sister, Jill, had been suggesting I bring Mark to SB and the Sansum clinic for evaluation and treatment. At this juncture of crisis, Jill and I connected and decided if I heard from Mark - that was the plan. To get him, by hook or by crook, to Santa Barbara. I prayed God would give us this chance, that He'd save Mark from himself this day and rescue him through a divine appointment in Santa Barbara.

And sure enough, some four or five agonizing hours later, Mark called. He was in Nevada somewhere heading… anywhere. He reiterated that he was at the end of his rope, but I knew he needed to hear my voice, that he was holding out hope that maybe this wasn't the end. I gave him everything I had, told him how much I loved and needed him, pleaded with him to come back and give Santa Barbara a try. After a long hour on the phone, he said he'd turn around and we'd head to the coast.

★★★★★

I don't know if Mark even got out of the car. I hopped in and drove us straight to Cottage Hospital in Santa Barbara. He was admitted and I remember when the elevator doors closed taking Mark away from me that I cried, - not before then, but right there in the hospital lobby. I called my pastor, suddenly overwhelmed with where I was and what I was doing. Was it the right thing subjecting Mark to worldly wisdom and practices of science and medicine? Psych units can be scary for so many reasons, in so many ways. I remember Brent said something that has stuck with me to this day. "Jody, truth can be found in many places." He reassured me that I was doing my best, had been seeking God every step of the way and could now leave Mark's well-being up to those who were sovereignly placed in our path for such a time as this. Praise God for that man who had sown into my life in so many varied seasons. For the first time in quite awhile, I was able to relinquish Mark's care to others and I headed for my sister's home to rest.

The first couple days were pretty rough. I visited Mark as long as time would allow, but he wasn't "Mark" so it was tough. He told me over lunch the first day that I really shouldn't show up without make-up as I looked like the side of a barn, whatever that meant.

35

(We actually chuckled about this later, but at the time it was painful. My feelings were hurt even though nothing about Mark was rational.) He also repeated something he'd voiced while lying in bed at my parent's home - that he didn't know if he loved me or ever had. It was probably all a like-minded China infatuation and most probably a mistake that we married. Oh my gosh.

Something happened while Mark was in the hospital that whisked me away for a few days. My grandfather died suddenly in Nebraska, and I, along with my family, flew out for the funeral to be with loved ones and my precious grandma. It was actually a very sweet time and helped lift me out of my own little world into a much bigger one where others were living and hurting and loving. In my absence, back in California, Mark's dad showed up and spent time with him. I knew this was a good thing, but at the same time, there were issues between Mark and his dad that might have complicated things. Nothing I could do about it; had to trust that God was in control.

By the time I returned, Mark had taken a turn for the better. Many have heard this story, but Mark and I felt like we found the silver bullet (or Wonka's golden ticket). A very reputable psychiatrist in town skipped all the guinea pig, trial and error stuff, and went straight to something potent: an MAO Inhibitor often prescribed as a last resort for atypical depression. After listening to Mark's history and all that he'd already tried, the doctor felt that Nardil was the way to go - risks, side effects and all.

And Mark chose life and went for it.

*****

The turnaround wasn't immediate, though all things considered, it was pretty quick. It was drastic to Mark. So many times he told friends he was better in three days. And I'm sure it seemed that way to him, so amazing was the change. And I was so danged relieved. I could take deep breaths. By the grace of God, we were alive again, and though I was cautiously optimistic about moving forward, I was equally anxious to put this hellish chapter behind us and *change the subject* as it were.

And we didn't wait long. Since it didn't seem wise to head

overseas at this point, Mark and I jumped at the chance to head back to Albuquerque at the invitation of his friend and pastor, Skip, to rejoin the church staff. It was such a vote of confidence and blessing from the Lord. And it seemed the right thing to do as we'd already resigned our positions in Lancaster and our bags were packed. We were rerouted from Hong Kong to New Mexico for the time being.

So sometime mid 1986, after one very hard year, we drove a few miles beyond Albuquerque and cozied up in a little mountain apartment on the same property where Mark had previously lived. I was euphoric. Mark was well and zooming; we were active in ministry once again, and I was living at the beautiful southern tip of the Rocky Mountains in Cedar Crest, New Mexico. God had let His people go and I was thankful.

HELLO NEW MEXICO

From the onset, Mark was the missions guy at Calvary. Having accumulated lots of overseas experience now, albeit short-term, this was an exciting season of development within the local church. We pretty much turned off the past year, plus, and plowed ahead with new relationships and activity. We were only too anxious to look forward.

When we first got back to Albuquerque, the church there had recently moved into a large sports facility and was in the middle of remodeling and expanding. I remember one little, crazy scare as Mark and I wandered the building greeting old friends and future coworkers that often creeps into my mind to this day. We were standing in front of one man's desk and chatting a bit with him when suddenly a full sentence of Mark's came out of his mouth all jumbled with words out of order and a bit slurred. If he purposed to say that string of words, I don't think he could have managed to muddle them up so thoroughly. Our friend looked up confused and Mark was just embarrassed, I think. I was concerned. Like I said, it was a little scare; it didn't happen again and Mark shrugged it off and put it at the very back of his brain, I'm certain. He was done with messed up minds and wasn't going to spend much time pondering what had just happened. I, on the other hand, though ready to move on, did ponder what was going on in Mark's head.

*****

This was a special season in our lives. We started a Missions Fellowship that grew to over 100 folks if all on the roster were

39

accounted for. Our meetings were filled with camaraderie as we learned what it meant to both go into the mission field and to send others. Some of the relationships built around that group of people have endured to this day. Our gang became known for hanging out at the ABQ airport as we had a commitment to showing up as often as possible when one of our co-laborers was heading out to or coming home from some Jesus designed destination. (I have some pretty funny pictures of the garb we'd sometimes wear for laughs.)

So many missionaries told Mark and me how meaningful and blessed our ministry was to them. In case you don't know, being a missionary can be lonely. There's a lot of tearing between two worlds and, unfortunately, too often, the sent ones can be somewhat forgotten, out-of-sight-out-of-mind. Mark and I made it our mission to insure this didn't happen on our watch. We worked hard at making sure our precious friends were cared for before, during, and after their mission stints.

Not too long following our ABQ arrival, we began planning for the church's first-ever School of Missions up at our Cedar Crest digs. A lot of prep went into this and Mark seemed to have endless energy for all that was required. The school, itself, entailed on-site housing (i.e. community living); three or four hours of teaching and equipping each morning; a work program every afternoon and various evening activities whether amongst our little school or at the church in town. What fun and what a challenge.

Something else we did regularly was to invite new found friends to our home for a meal. We were really determined to know folks and be in relationship, so usually once a week we'd have a little Sunday afternoon BBQ or potluck or pizza-fest at our place. I thoroughly enjoyed these small gatherings. We were running on all cylinders.

As I said, Mark had endless energy. But sometimes I'd wear out. And sometimes, I longed for a quiet, peaceful few hours - just the two of us. Whatever time off we did have was often spent running errands to be ready for the next activity. And there was this little nagging worry in the back of my mind that Mark was too on. I mean he just kept going and going and going. I remember one time, as our school was prepping to head to Mexico for an outreach that he stayed up most of the night working on a bus which was probably better served by a real mechanic. I was annoyed. Or maybe mad was the better adjective. I didn't think it good for Mark to be pushing so hard.

Although, it didn't really appear a push. At the time I thought perhaps it was my own lens and disposition of low energy. Maybe Mark was just healthy; maybe he was revitalized to his normal after a bad year of abnormal. Truthfully I was churning inside. I wanted him to slow down; I wanted him to rest and have rest time. On the other hand, I was still so gratefully aware of the bullet we dodged, that I didn't talk much about it with Mark. We did have a few conversations, or maybe I gave a few speeches, on the liabilities of endless activity. For my part, I warned Mark that he needed to take care of himself, if not for his own good - for mine. I couldn't slide into the abyss of another downward-cycle-season. But why should we? We'd discovered the wonder drug.

*****

About four years into our marriage, in the fall of 1988, Mark and I got the wonderful news that we were pregnant. We were ready and excited. (Somewhere in our first year, I miscarried. As anyone who has experienced this knows, it's not easy. Emotions go haywire. Mark's did right alongside mine. He was a bit crazed at the idea of being a dad sooner than planned, yet guilt ridden that his health issues might have played a role in my miscarrying. I didn't realize how deep that fear went until the elation of pregnancy #2 presented and Mark was able to relax as one trimester glided smoothly to the next.)

*****

While I was pregnant, Mark took a team from Albuquerque to China. It was a great thing in that Mark had maintained communication and relationship with our friends overseas all the while he was engaged in a little different ministry in New Mexico. He would always say his "first love" - after Jesus and me - was China. It was a hard thing in that he traveled without me for the first time and I cried when he left. I went to California to stay with my family, so that was a treat, but still it was difficult for me to see Mark taking off across the ocean alone.

41

He fared well, I fared well. And over the years, it was just the first of many trips he made on his own.

*****

In January 1989, our home burned to the ground. You'd think if something was going to rattle my vulnerable husband, that would have done it. But he hardly flinched.

About 4:00 AM, asleep in our cozy little mountain apartment, our cat, Bogie, began making a ruckus. Finally, in distress, he got our attention and Mark and I awoke to flames licking up the side of our two story bedroom window. By the time we got our heads wrapped around what was happening, there was no chance for grabbing belongings. Mark did take a fire extinguisher to the flame outside our kitchen door, but the sizeable fire was way beyond deterrence. I managed to grab Bogie after pulling him out from under the guest bed and we threw on winter coats over our pj's as we scrambled out the front door and down some old wooden steps to safety. It was such a fluke fire. Here it was the middle of winter; pipes had frozen and broken that night leaving an ice skating rink surrounding much of the building. Firefighters, as a result, had no water pressure and no ability to hose down the rapidly destroying flames. Mark and I, likely in shock, sat on a berm near our home and watched our possessions disappear before our eyes. If it wasn't such a bummer, it would have been funny. Firemen were slip sliding all over the place; it was like a silent comedy eerie in the predawn light.

There were six of us affected by the fire: Mark and I, a young couple and baby home on furlough from the mission field, and a single young man. A few things were extracted from a couple areas before the flames totally engulfed the building, but for the most part, the facility was rendered a total loss by the fire inspectors. Although rental insurance covered the others because they were temporary residents, Mark and I - by another fluke - were unable to benefit from the insurance claim as we were deemed permanent ones, a company loophole. We didn't own a lot, hadn't accumulated much in our wandering four plus years; still we lost some treasures and some things that were foundational to homebuilding. I remember being oh so sad about losing the first toy our yet unborn child had received - a gift from Asia.

42

There was much for which to be thankful. No one was hurt. Friends rallied and loved on all of us. Perspectives were righted; values adjusted. I realized afresh that God is funny sometimes - I had recently finished reading Mother Theresa's biography and was most mindful about her two sets of clothes: the one she was wearing and the one she would change into while the other was laundered. Wow. Think that wasn't sobering? And then, suddenly, I had only my pajamas and a winter coat (covered with cat hair, I might add).

Within hours of the fire, Skip took us clothes shopping after treating us to breakfast at a happening restaurant. (Surely in our coats and pj's we were deemed homeless folks blessed by a magnanimous pastor.) For a while, all of our worldly goods were in a few brown paper bags. We stayed with Skip and his wife, Lenya, for a week or so while wrapping our heads around our circumstances, then we were set up to house sit for a stint until we were able to get our feet back under us. It wasn't bad, but it wasn't ideal either, me being pregnant and all. It wasn't exactly restful living in a house not my home. But still we were thankful that God had gone before us and provided all we needed.

When my birthday rolled around - the first of April - Mark surprised me by bringing my dad, mom and grandpa out to Albuquerque for a visit. Guess he figured I needed a little family boost and it was really so thoughtful of him. Mark was a rock through this entire fire ordeal. He laughed quite a bit and had me joining in as he talked of "always wanting to get rid of junk." He joked that God just accomplished this desire of his so much more efficiently than we ever could. Truly it was just not a very big deal to Mark and not so much to me either, apart from a few precious losses. In hindsight, Mark's strength in this season lent definition to his illness. At times, he was invincible.

*****

The next six months were not easy being vagabonds, me being pregnant and changes happening on the job and ministry front. God totally took care of us, but again, it wasn't easy. For several reasons, Mark ended up resigning his post at the church and we incorporated a new ministry - Life to the Nations. By this time Mark had built many strong relationships overseas and stateside and was ready to go at the missions aspect of his calling full-time. We rented a little office - I can still see the wall maps - and Mark was a happy camper.

After a few house-sitting stays, we eventually rented an apartment in town and finally had a place to call home again. My mom had helped me do some consignment store shopping so our furniture and household bases were covered. Mark, Bogie and I moved into a nice little two bedroom apartment with a view of the Sandia Mountains (which was important coming down from those same mountains to live in town).

And finally, July came. Mark and I celebrated our five year anniversary and Levi Morgan Macallister was born. He came under circumstances other than we'd planned, but it was a new season, and hey!

I remember feeling a little apprehensive in the aftermath of our fire. I wondered how Mark would fare with all the stressors of upheaval and change, new responsibilities and more required dependence on God than ever for our livelihood. And it wasn't that he never manifested the normal responses to such things, but that's the point. His responses were within the normal continuum. And I honestly wasn't sure what life would look like with Levi expanding our little twosome. After my earlier miscarriage, I knew Mark questioned whether or not he was made to be a father.

*****

But Levi's arrival dispelled all that and the month or two after his birth are some of the sweetest days in memory. - What I recall most is Mark bringing Levi to me in the mornings so I wouldn't have to get out of bed for early AM feedings. I think Mark was awestruck. That this beautiful boy would be his - healthy and whole - was beyond his wildest hopes.

One thing Mark and I talked a lot about before having kids was that they were to be a part of our lives entering in to our lifestyle; we wouldn't overhaul our routines and goals to simply accommodate them. (Over the years this determination ebbed and flowed.) First example: 10 days after Levi was born, after saying goodbye to my parents who were out for the grandbaby welcoming, Mark and I loaded up our car and the three of us drove to Denver for a National Vineyard conference. Some folks thought we were nuts, and maybe we were, but we didn't know any better and it worked. We just did what we were about.

Sometime later in the fall, we were invited to attend a Broncos game in Phoenix with some friends. We packed a diaper bag, dressed Levi in loyal Bronco orange and boarded an airplane to sit out in the hot Arizona sunshine all afternoon. I will say Levi overheated a bit on the way home, required a strip down and some cool air for the duration of the trip. Live and learn.

As weeks went on, our season in Albuquerque seemed to be changing. Though nothing was amiss really, Mark and I sensed a pulling back to California. When we had returned to Albuquerque, our purpose was clear. Now it was a little fuzzier. What we were doing - focusing on missions locally and abroad - was good, but not necessarily Albuquerque-bound. Things were going on back in So Cal that we didn't want to miss and didn't need to miss due to our autonomous ministry nature. Plus all our family was out west.

Though feeling a bit like a bouncing ball, before Levi hit year one, the Macallisters were headed back to California.

ANOTHER CALIFORNIA SEASON

This time, we really walked by faith. We had no job to return to, no home set up for instant start, yet it felt right. Mark and I were excited to plug back in to our local church and all that was happening there. We were glad to have grandparents around for Levi's sake. (Mark's grandparents played a more significant role in his life than his parents; mine had lived two days away from my little nuclear family and I missed them terribly. So for Levi to have grandparents near was a big deal.)

When we first got back to Lancaster, we stayed with my parents off and on for awhile. We had friends who offered us their home in the expansive, big sky and rugged Leona Valley while they traveled some. Mark found work with the US Census Bureau and walked many streets (and collected quite a few stories to coincide with those walks). Not knowing what the future held, he went back to school and worked on a teaching license. These were the days when teachers were in short supply, so positions were crying to be filled.

For a good while, Mark substitute taught at various schools throughout the Antelope Valley. It wasn't long before he came home one afternoon and said we'd never send one of our kids to a public school in LA County. Tells you a little about the realities of public education and how Mark felt about being a part of it.

It also was meaningful that Mark said *one of the kids*. We were pregnant with #2! The best surprise of our lives, but still caught a little off guard as Levi was not quite a year old when we discovered I was pregnant once again. Amazingly, considering all Mark's reservations about being a dad, he was more excited and at peace with the very near arrival of another baby than I was. Although he never wanted to know our second's gender (I did), he so smoothly had transitioned into being a daddy that one more little body just made him all happy.

Things were coming together for us on the home front, too. We moved into a cute little house, the Date House, where several church folks had lived and cycled through previous to our turn there. It was so nice to have a place to call home again.

Sometime during this transition, Mark went from crazy, to crazier still, in the job market. We were very grateful, however. Mark applied for and was granted a position in a lock-down school for juvenile delinquents. Although I never did attend one of his classes - I don't know if that was even possible - I had the feeling that Mark found a little niche at that school and was anointed for the job. I know he was a good teacher and made a difference in many a lonely boy's life. Sometimes he'd come home with hair-raising stories of fights breaking out in his classroom. When this occurred Mark would have to trigger an alarm for armed security to rush in and sort things out; Mark was not to touch a student - ever. One time he did in the excitement of the moment and we were a little worried for a few days of what the repercussions might be. I think God must have covered him because, other than a little reprimand, Mark came out unscathed, job intact. - So there were the fights and times when Mark wanted to enter the fray and dole out beatings to the perpetrators. Other times he wished he could bring a kid home to live with us for awhile, so heartbroken he'd be over some boy's story. Mark became very attached to a few of his students and I know he was always thinking if it weren't for Jesus, he could have been one of them.

*****

April 1, 1991 - Bree Ariel Macallister was born. On my birthday!

As I became more and more huge and as Bree's due date of March 27th approached, I suddenly had this downer of an idea that she might be late and show up on the fateful April Fools' Day - the birthday I hated growing up. It was no fun being teased at school about being born a fool or having double

48

the jokes pulled on you just because it was your birthday. I began praying that my sweet little daughter would show up on time or any day other than April 1st. But, alas, it wasn't meant to be.

I had a Jewish doctor who was both a faithful Sabbath observer and a committed vacationer and would be totally unavailable here and there around April 1st. If he was to deliver our baby and she didn't show up by March 31st, she would be induced and arrive April 1st. Done deal.

Mark was great with all of it. Come March 30th, on a rainy/sleety night, he talked me into believing tomorrow would be an awesome day to induce labor and my birthday would be the perfect day to bring baby #2 into the world. He was a great birthing coach, once more, and got a little teary-eyed with me as we entered the sacred hours of childbirth again. (He was partly identifying with my pain, I'm sure, but he also was rejoicing that he was good with being a dad now.)

He was a little freaked to have a daughter, though he wanted her badly. He'd never had any sisters. His mom-relationship left much to be desired. He just didn't know how to treat a little girl. Ahhh well. He did fine.

We had a short, sweet little season as in the aftermath of Levi's birth. Mark went to work every day and came home to a tired, but happy mommy, and two little munchkins, - one ready to tear around horseback on his daddy, the other swinging sweetly in her crank up chair swing.

Unfortunately, the season wasn't long enough and suddenly, another cycle was upon us.

*****

Things were stressful at work. Of that fact, no one doubted. Being in a locked classroom - in a larger lockdown facility, by description - told the tale. There were politics involved at the local, state, and federal level. There were egos in play and personalities hardened to the plight of young boys behind bars. Then there was such anger, bitterness, brokenness and, sometimes, demonic influence in the classroom that it's no wonder Mark's health wore thin.

He began getting cluster migraines. Neither of us had ever heard of them before and we didn't link them with any of his other health issues. He'd done so well for so long through so many other stressful scenarios that we truly thought this was something different, not the vicious black hole descending.

For anyone who's ever experienced migraines before, you'd figure one exploding on the heels of another would be daunting. One right after another after another would be debilitating.

So at first, we didn't know what was going on. Mark was familiar with an occasional migraine in the past, but nothing like this. This was scary. - The pain grew so bad that Mark thought maybe he was having a brain bleed and we rushed to the emergency room where we first heard the term *cluster migraine*. It was a relief on the one hand (as opposed to hearing you just had a stroke or something exploded in your head), but cluster migraines are hard to control. Sometimes they have to just run their course and Mark's course wasn't a quick one. We were at the hospital a couple times, so severe was the pain, so exhausting the duration. (One time Mark could have died in the ER. He was almost given Demerol to which he was highly allergic. A nurse hadn't read his chart and was in a big hurry to get his pain under control. Oops. Good thing Mark was cognitive enough to catch the blooper.)

Mark couldn't move most days, let alone get out of bed and go to work. He wanted to. This wasn't depression or anxiety at this point. Just some crazy ailment from left field that took Mark down for the count. When it went on and on, day in, day out, Mark became concerned for his little family's well-being and his lack of ability to bring home a paycheck. - I honestly don't remember how it all worked out, but somehow there was some disability involved and factored into a workman's comp claim and the powers that be were okay with it. Praise God.

*****

So next cycle was made manifest as the cluster migraines went on and on and the wonderful, silver bullet of a depression/anxiety med was dangerously interactive with the migraine helps. And being that we didn't know any better and had transitioned a couple years back to a different doctor who wasn't nearly so impressed with the MAO Inhibitor, Mark began to wean off the Nardil so as to try something less complicated and less contraindicative with other meds.

And we revisited hell.

I've been writing for six months now, Mark. Remembering and smiling; remembering and weeping. I miss you. But I wouldn't ask you back, not when I know how hard life was for you here. Not when I know how good it is for you there, with Jesus.

I'm well. God is taking good care of me. But it's a strange world I live in now. For the longest time it was so disorienting. I think I understand the "denial" stage of grief although all the while knowing you were gone. It just wasn't possible you weren't coming back the next day or the next. And then as days wore on and I moved forward, it still seemed odd that I was doing this on my own. You always encouraged me to do things I didn't think I could do, but really I did so little without you, at least without the thought of you alongside me doing it all.

Our marriage wasn't easy, but isn't it amazing how God redeems everything and I remember, now, mostly the sweet times? What a gift. 27 years of knowing and loving you, hard times and all. And there was many a season when I didn't think I'd make it, didn't think I could stay, but of all things I'm happy about - I'm most glad that I did. I stayed. By the grace of God. Thank you, Jesus, that You walked with us because we couldn't walk our days without You.

In The Middle

BOUT TWO

There seems no end to the side effects or fiery darts that come with mental illness. Mark said one time that he'd much rather battle cancer or some fatal disease than depression and anxiety and all their tentacles. I'm sure the former aren't easy either, but they're a little more definable and acceptable, if I can say it that way.

So we weaned off the Nardil and the guinea pig trials began. All to no avail. I had a little boy, almost two, romping the house. A baby girl needing her baby routine, and a husband back in bed. The cluster migraines hung around for a long while and after circling the wagons several times, one doctor wanted to prescribe Nardil for the headaches, saying it was among the most helpful meds for such ailments. Geez. We'd just gotten rid of the Nardil.

The build up and weaning off process was excruciating for Mark. Apart from what I can only call 'mental anguish,' other strange things happened. Like the day when Mark's body temperature was all out of whack (which happened frequently). Sometimes a hot bath would help, and even though we were smack in the middle of a summer day, Mark crawled into the bath tub with all the energy he had. After being there for only ten or fifteen minutes, I heard him call me and went to find him balled up with his hands all gnarled and stiff. He was scared to death. Now what? I called a nurse line at the hospital and was told Mark's electrolytes were likely off and I needed to spoon him salt water until his limbs and hands could relax. A simple solution and thankfully the right one, but what the heck?

We had some wonderful friends who walked this season with us and spent many hours at our home keeping me company and sitting with Mark - often through the night hours when nightmares were frequent and the darkness, lonely.

But no matter how hard we tried to avoid it, Mark ended up in the hospital again.

This hospitalization is all a little fuzzy in my brain, probably because I had two kids to tend to and was doing my best to keep *normal* running at home. I believe Mark was inpatient for about two weeks during which time the Nardil was reintroduced and slowly but surely, Mark was reintroduced as well. He showed up once again.

On the heels of his hospital discharge, I have a poignant memory: Mark and I leaving our babies behind with my parents for a few days while he and I drove up the coast for a little R&R. It seemed important that we do it, and I wanted to for that reason, but I was also dying a little inside because of our reality and why we were doing it. It was painful.

*****

California's Central Coast was gorgeous. Big Sur and Cambria, Morro Bay and Monterrey breathtaking. We drove along slowly taking it all in, breathing deeply, - glad once again for restoration and life. For rescue and release. But also along the way, there was much pondering. Mostly silent. Neither of us had many words to regurgitate what had just happened - again. Neither of us wanted to project what it meant for our future. For our kids.

And Mark still wasn't 100%. We were in that season of quiet, gentle, baby steps - learning to walk once more. We did a lot of nothing, beach wandering, window shopping, reading, whispering...

Somewhere along the way, my calm demeanor rebelled and I became defiant in my inner woman; I determined that life was going to change. Mark would start taking excellent care of himself with my help, and we would never mess with the Nardil again. We would go home, start fresh and be well. Period.

*****

Once more, slowly but surely as Mark caught his stride, life became full again. He remained off work awhile, but we got more involved at church leading a home fellowship and participating with the missions group. Plus we had our little folks at home - now three and one - and this season with them was precious.

Over the course of Mark's illness, our lead pastor and friend, Brent, was fighting his own battles - first melanoma and then esophageal cancer. It was a tough time for our Body and stretching for the staff (including the Macs back in the loop) as we learned more acutely what it meant to be family. One thing Mark did to fill a gap in Brent's stead was to head to Siberia for a couple weeks. Our church had slowly shifted its overseas focus from China and Bible deliveries to church planting in Russia's far reaches. Although it wasn't a personal calling for Mark, still his heart was for folks in dark places and Siberia fit the bill. I remember him packing his suitcases, readying for the temperatures he never encountered in Asia.

I can't comment much on that trip, not having gone, but I know Mark was a blessing to folks from our Body who were planting there. That role was in Mark's heart: to be an encouragement to missionaries overseas and, over the years, he was able to fulfill that desire many times.

On the home front, as Brent's life became more fragile, Mark took a rotating shift sitting at Brent's bedside praying for and over him until he ultimately went Home to be with Jesus. (Brent was amazing in dying. He truly, gently took the church with him through the valley of the shadow, - pastoring and pointing to Jesus. Such a bittersweet journey.)

Following Brent's move, our church went through a lot of transition, some of which launched our little family into one of my favorite life seasons.

HELLO RANCH

David, our new pastor, asked the Macallisters to move up to that beautiful property in the mountains - where our wedding was held - and lead the Ranch Ministries. And I thought I was in Heaven. I think this opportunity had been my dream for a long time. I loved the mountain setting; I loved the whole idea of ministry school. I loved that, once again, God had raised Mark up out of the pit to leadership under full disclosure (on Mark's part) and full endorsement (on David's part). It blesses me, still, that one pastor/leader after another - knowing full well Mark's propensity to some sort of crazy imbalance - still recognized in him leadership qualities and character. If that doesn't speak of God's amazing irrevocable gifts, I don't know what does.

Although our Date Street house had been our first family home, it was with hardly any sadness that we packed up our meager belongings and headed up the Liebre Mountain to our next destination.

*****

It wasn't a glamorous beginning although I loved every minute. The Hanta-virus was big in 1993; remember the deer mice and all the scary reports on television? The Macallisters were allotted a double wide mobile home that had been sitting empty nearby the Ranch construction graveyard. (So imagine critter stomping grounds.) Actually Mark and I had made several pre-move trips up the mountain to scour down, on hands and knees, our new home with bleach. It wasn't fun, but boy did we have a spanking-clean house when we moved in, mice-be-gone. And we had a big, furry cat to take over from there so infiltrators were greatly minimized.

I remember waking up the first morning after our move and walking down to the Community kitchen with Levi and Bree, my heart soaring with the reality of my life and the goodness of Jesus. It was a gorgeous, warm sunny day. School had not yet begun so people were scarce and the kids and I enjoyed just wandering around the empty buildings and grounds. I wish I could have gotten into Levi's and Bree's little brains then to know how they were processing their new digs. I'm pretty sure Levi was already wearing his cowboy boots so that tells me something. And Bree was little; it was a bit of a hike for her to waddle on down to the kitchen. Adventure!

For a couple weeks or so, it was just us Macs and the other Ranch staff preparing for the Fall School of Ministry (SOM) - 1993. Mark and I worked on his little office which overlooked the ministry area but was, in reality, more of a recreational venue complete with fire-pit and basketball hoop all at the dining hall front entrance. Most of my Ranch memories are of spending hours around that center circle/fire pit, soaking in sun and fellowship by day, relaxing and sharing lives, by night, with the many folks who sojourned up the mountain.

Mark's office wasn't fancy. We're talking rural, ranch facilities built in the 1950's maybe, and those were the newer units. Some of the original buildings, Spanish style, went up in the early 1930's. Cowboys, movie stars, oil tycoons and politicians frequented this Los Angeles escape back in the day. But, I stray... Mark's office was little with rickety windows, but he had a view of the action and gathering of folks all day long from his desk. We so enjoyed setting up shop for him there.

Mark was thorough in everything he did. He needed order around him to function well and I used to chuckle at him straightening paper clips and rubber bands if aberrant supplies were discovered in his desk drawers. Books were categorized on shelves, file trays were labeled for efficiency. Now this is not to say he always knew where to find everything. He had a great system down but could rarely find his keys or reading glasses or that fat pen best for lefties! If anyone needed anything from his office, though, rummaging to find it wouldn't take long.

So we set up office and we set up house. Our home was a little jaunt up and away from the community living/ministry area but totally a doable walk. And it was a sweet little double wide mobile home, all cozy and country looking. The kids each had their own bedroom. We bought Levi some real cowboy-appropriate, early American bunk beds. Bree got her own double bed, all girly. As the years went by and the grounds were improved on (the construction graveyard disappeared; grass, trees and landscaping went in), our views from the living room and kitchen were amazing. In one direction we could see miles off to the Tehachapi Mountains, another to the sand volleyball court and grassy guest-cottage lawn; and yet another up the mountain towards the swimming hole/reservoir. Seriously as I see it all again, now in my mind, I do believe I got to live in Heaven, prematurely, awhile. The setting was a dream come true for me.

*****

About the time the Macallisters were ready to welcome our first School of Ministry students, Levi started Kindergarten and that created another dynamic in our lives. Being that we were about 45 minutes from town, it was decided that the kids and I would stay with my parents after church on Sundays through Tuesday afternoons each week. We chose to home school in partnership with our church program so Levi attended school Mondays and Tuesdays, and then Wednesdays through Fridays, we studied at home. (Remember Mark saying no way to public school for our kids a couple years back? Good thing we weren't counting on it, because life on the Ranch would have been stressful if we could even pull it off with two wee ones in tow back and forth to town every day.)

So week one for Levi began in Lancaster at "Boppa & Gawa's" house. Mark came in for the big day and we made a family appearance at the school; so sweet. Reports afterwards, first day and ongoing, indicated that Levi preferred sitting by his teacher at lunch, and many girls in his class were attracted to him immediately. Smiling.

Bree and I did the town thing while Levi was in class. Often she got to stay with her grandparents while I did the errand running and that seemed to work for everyone. I wasn't toting a toddler; she wasn't fussing at being toted. Boppa and Gawa got to enjoy her (most of the time). Mark was the only one really missing out and I could hardly call *never having to come to town* missing out. He did miss us though and I wish I'd have recognized that building up before it ultimately became known two or three years later.

INTERNATIONAL SCHOOL OF MINISTRY

Airport runs. Suitcases everywhere. Room assignments. Notes and candies, hotel style, on student bedding. Unpacking. Roommate bonding. Dining room greetings and first meals. Fire-pit gatherings. Students from Australia, England, Sweden, Germany, Norway, Canada, France, New Zealand, South Africa, and all over the US. It was so fun.

And some of the best of the best teachers inside and outside the Vineyard movement coming to train, teach and hang with us. God, You restored Mark for this. Amazing.

★★★★★

Rancho Corona del Valle. It was very different in 1993 than today. Now one can pay $140 a night to stay there and take part in local hiking or horseback riding or gun club escapades. Artists check it out as I hear the lighting/shadowing on the Tehachapi Mountains is phenomenal to the painter-eye. Folks wanting a *different* kind of get-away would enjoy the reclusivity of the place. But I tell ya, nothing can compare to the God-Presence: the beauty, majesty and sacredness, of those SOM years. Life together.

Our little family of four was fully immersed in a unique international atmosphere; I think our first student body had 21 individuals, varying ages, from all over the globe. Every first day of School we'd kick off our season together with a big barbecue in the ministry area and just get acquainted. It didn't take long, mind you, when studying, working, eating, and rooming together as the students did, but still the first day jitters were often present - or was that the jet-lag many were experiencing?

Mark's typical day began up and at his office by 7:45 AM or so before class started at 8:00. He would usually start each school off with an overview of what to expect, etc, and do some interactive stuff the first few days before guest speakers began to roll in. Most of the time Mark sat in on classes - or at least he did for the first two or three years while everything was new to him. Otherwise he'd be in his office planning for whatever was next on the calendar, - whether that be nightly events, outreaches, or just the daily juggle. He was never lacking things to do.

Class would end by noon and we'd all gather for lunch in the dining hall or ministry area; Levi and Bree loved it as their mornings were spent homeschooling up the hill. They couldn't wait to join the gang. (I don't think I'm overly biased in saying the students enjoyed them equally as well.)

After lunch there was a four hour work program where the students were assigned jobs around the facilities and grounds ranging from housekeeping and meal prep to gardening and maintenance. If our kids loved the community meals, they were ecstatic about work program. Little, pudgy, four year old Bree on a step stool in the kitchen stirring huge bowls of cake batter. Levi, complete in Superman attire with cowboy boots (that boy!) supervising the grounds crew!

Mark didn't do it every day, because he had his own job to do, but periodically he'd join in with the work groups and labor alongside them. He believed that was important and he enjoyed doing it, - hanging out with the students in these times. Again, another opportunity for life together.

I had split devotion going on all the time at The Ranch. On the one hand, I wanted to be a part of every minute of the learning, stretching, joyous student experience. On the other, I was protective of my little family, concerned that it might be swallowed up by the community to the exclusion of our own Mac-life. It was always a delicate balance. (I tried to incorporate some family time: a meal or two at home routinely, Saturday morning home leisure and chores, occasional off-Ranch outings - just us. Sometimes it worked and other times it didn't.)

*****

So we started at the Ranch late summer 1993. We did two schools a year, spring and fall, and in between, there were retreats and weekend events that took place on our mountain paradise. The seasons rolled along, one after another, with joy abounding as we met new people and grew together. International and American Jesus-Family coming to soak up an experience with the Lord like none other.

One highlight for me as a mom, besides the community living aspect, was participating in the SOM outreaches. I still remember how I felt time and time again when we'd load up the 15 passenger vans and trailers and hit the highway. We'd wind down Pine Canyon Road and spill on to I-5 and I'd see all these cars with people headed to work or school or who knows where, and I'd think: *How did I get so blessed to be riding off with my family and these great people to serve Jesus when everyone else was doing ordinary life?* Seriously. It blew my mind every time. And Levi and Bree were as awed and excited as I was to be adventuring with all their "friends." Mark was happy to have us along and to be providing his family with rich experiences most people would only ever hear about. Ahhh Lord. I marvel.

We'd go to Mexico/Baja California and work at orphanages for a week or two. Or we'd serve at churches there, helping with children's ministries and the like. We'd go to San Francisco, to Haight Ashbury and worship with the homeless or runaway street kids who flocked to the big cities on their spiritual journeys. We went to East LA and came alongside believers already laboring on behalf of gang infested and impoverished neighborhoods. We'd do the work and we'd also play - enjoying Baja beaches, SF cruisin', Ben & Jerry's, and . . . little in LA actually. (My kids got to see their dad in action, leading and loving a huge blended family, so in his groove to train others to serve - the goal of the SOM.)

Back on the Ranch, I was equally wowed by God's goodness to the Macallisters. A lot of what we did was simply live with the family of God. I was always amazed that when we surveyed the students at the end of each school, the number one highlight/"stretch-er" of their time with us was Community Living. Above any specific teaching brought by amazing men and women, above any outpouring of the Holy Spirit even, - living communally was what challenged lives to change and look more like Jesus. (Many books are out there on the topic of Community Living; I could write one, myself, with all the observation, experience and pondering I've done on the subject. Don't get me started!)

Providing an American experience for internationals - though not mentioned in the SOM syllabus - was part of Ranch fun and I have some memorable holiday pictures in my mind. Thanksgiving, particularly, was always special. Staff and students, alike, took part in cooking, decorating and participating in the sweet celebrating of God's gracious goodness in our lives. At Christmastime, there was caroling and precious plays staged by whatever children were there at the Ranch with their parents. Easters meant trekking to the Punchbowl a few years - up at 3AM to caravan from town in time for sunrise at another beauteous location. There were costume parties that coincided with Halloween and/or Harvest. One year Mark and I won best couple costume: the Princess and the Pea. Can you imagine?

Another really special part of each School was the weekly evening fellowship where each student would share his or her testimony of meeting the Lord and of present testimony: what God was up to in their lives now. These were times when you got to hear the hearts of the Community, brothers and sisters. Some stories were amazing and miraculous, some heart-breaking, some sweet and simple, but all proclamations of God's reach and faithfulness towards His beloved created.

Now the hard part about the Schools was saying goodbye. There were many tears at the end of each session knowing that for most, we'd never see each other again this side of Heaven. Family relationships, some hard fought for, were established over the course of three or four months only to be separated at completion of the calendar. It was often heart-wrenching. And I think for all the wonderful, awesome experiences the Macallisters were allowed, there is still some residue of not-so-wonderful, especially in my kids. The entering and leaving of treasured people in their lives was maybe too difficult at times for young hearts. On the other hand, today they're better than most people I know at genuinely loving their friends and sharing deep and committed life with them. God works all things together for good.

*****

School seasons were intensive (and intense) packing so much teaching, training, outreach, community living, and all the emotion that goes with them, into a relatively short period of time. The alternate seasons were comparatively light-weight though often just as busy. Activities and events were turned over weekly and community mostly meant the Ranch staff. We'd have weekly Bible Studies and meetings; we'd share at least one meal a day. We'd participate, to the degree we were invited, in the various meetings held as part of retreats, conferences, etc.

Our Ranch staff became our immediate family in many ways over the years. Though its members changed at times, for the most part, the core folks were longer termed and that helped with some of the hard-goodbye stuff.

I love, to this day, the relational connections Mark and I made during our Ranch years. I loved the privilege of playing a support role for the schools, first to Mark and then to the staff and students. I loved being a wife and mommy in the midst of our community. It was all so rich and fulfilling. Yet I was nervous sometimes. I knew I needed reprieves and down times. I knew Mark needed them; we needed them as a family. So sometimes, when life started tilting sideways a little, when I'd feel anxious inside, I'd go to a happy place…

I found solace (or went crazy) in the Ranch garden.

PLANTING, WATERING, WEEDING

One thing I could never settle in my mind, where Mark's health was concerned, was what was good for him and what was bad. As our time at the Ranch took off, he jumped in with passion and fervor. He was great in his job description. I was proud of him administrating the schools, mentoring/ministering to students, teaching topics in his areas of expertise. He was truly a Servant Leader, all would agree, managing staff, students and liaison between the church and School. So that was all good. The bad was the push, the endless hours, the irregular sleep, the always on. I used to think he was simply a hopeless workaholic. Years later I understood more clearly, it was a manic, of sorts, in the cyclothymic rhythm. When I would try to convince, when I would nag and plead (not best methods) for some down time, a day off, I was often met with resistance or any agreement would be lost in actions a day or two later. Needless to say, this took a toll on our marriage. And I would doubt my heart and my motives for asking for more of Mark for myself. I mean we did sign up for ministry and I was so thankful he was seemingly healthy. I hated to complain about him working. That he was able to work was a gift beyond measure. So my own confusion about how to live our lives was often significant. (And then there was the whole *pastor's wife* deal. Wasn't I to be totally selfless?)

So I had this therapeutic project at the Ranch: a garden. I wasn't the creator of the garden (though I did help some with the planting) but I might have been its #1 visitor spending time at least once a day watering and pulling weeds and harvesting some yummies for evening meals. Mark and I had had a wonderful garden at our home in town and I learned working in it brought peace and was good for times of meditating and dialing down. Everyone's probably heard many analogies of gardening pertaining to wellness; I was sucking life out of them in reality.

Somewhere around 1995, 1996, things became rough. Preceding the worst of it though, as Mark's and my relationship became more and more strained, God led me to do a slow-paced, intensive reading through the Bible. I took one chapter a day so it took me three years to complete, but again, this fellowship with the Lord was critical to my own sanity and health. By the time we were full-bore into Mark's next cycle, I was well into my Bible study where I read a chapter and journaled about a Spirit-highlighted verse each day. The essence of Jesus and His Word being my Daily Bread became so real to me. (I'm tempted to repeat that discipline, but I know it was so God-breathed at the time, a repeat wouldn't compare.)

I planted the Word and I planted the Word and I watered the Word deep, deep in my heart. Oh how I needed Him. My marriage was swirling out of control. The Macallisters were living community, in a fish bowl (notice the not so subtle shift away from *paradise*) and I didn't know what to do about it. My emotions were taut and I shifted to survival mode.

*****

This cycle manifested differently. We didn't end up in the hospital. Mark didn't get cluster migraines or such deep depression that he couldn't move. He was sickly, though, spending a day here and there in bed, and he couldn't sleep consistently. He did have a very hard time waking up in the mornings once he finally was able to nod off maybe at 4 or 5 AM. And he was angry.

I don't know if I was just the closest target or if our wrestling reality made me particularly ugly, but we couldn't get along to save our lives. I suppose we should have stepped out of our roles and left the Ranch, but at the time, the Ranch seemed our salvation too. Mark had a semblance of self-control when he was functioning as Ranch Director. I chalked up his intense focus and the responsibility he felt towards his job as factors that kept him, at least, on the edge of the storm rather than in its rage. He kept plowing through, and again, I was hesitant to stomp my foot and tell him to stop. What would the inactivity, the lack of purposed focus do? Such a quandary.

72

It wasn't that Mark didn't recognize the problems. He did as well as I did. But he would say - whether he felt it to be totally true or not - that the problems were mine. And as I said earlier, I was a contributor for sure. Reasoning became pleading and nagging on my part at times. I was angry, too, that we were living our dream life yet there was this huge black blight in the middle of it. I didn't think our kids were getting enough of Mark; I knew I wasn't. (I have a hard time saying these things even now. I feel whiney. But others, smarter than I, have since breathed life, and I trust, truth, into me. Mark and I lived in cyclical seasons of thick fog, difficult for anyone to navigate because they weren't totally sane.)

My Bible study/daily quiet time was a life-giving I.V., watering a despairing soul. Garden weeding occurred at some point, when I began seeing a counselor who helped me walk through my pain and the disillusionment that was my life. I went through the Christian 12 Step Program. I talked through all my confusion and feelings of failure and helplessness. I wore the idea that somehow I should have been able to fix our problems or prevent them, *if only I* . . . and it plagued me. It was hard to reconcile that our problem was beyond me or us. What do you do with that except to accept and forgive and trust Jesus for your next breath - just like in everything. Slowly but surely, I got a handle on moving forward and working on my marriage - the parts that I could. Before that point, I wasn't sure Mark and I would survive this cycle, so wounded was I in the process. So done in most every way.

To add crazy to crazy, as the typical 18 months began drawing to a close, Mark's *angry* began to lift and he evened out emotionally and was oh so sorry for all he put his family through. He joined me in counseling and we went together, and separately, trying to put the pieces back together. And this was a good thing, but, big groan. I hated it, - that we were in this place. I hated it for me and the kids, and I hated it for Mark. It was like a demon had free access to him every fifth year for 12 to 18 months, - would beat him up within an inch of his life and then laughingly flit away until the next time. Just when Mark's confidence would be somewhat intact again and our lives would be cautiously optimistic and we'd step out one more time, I would scream inside, "What the hell, Lord?"

*****

Amazingly we finished out the Ranch experience on a good note. The cycle came and went smack in the middle and for this I am thankful. This way my memory of our years there is not totally marred; that Ranch season still ranks top on my favorites list and I wouldn't trade it for anything.

NEXT STOP: THE BAY AREA

At some point, Mark and I knew we'd run our Ranch course and it was time to move on. Originally Ranch Directors were only to stay on for three years, so taxing was community living thought to be on families. I suppose it's true. Mark felt the stress of managing a ginormous family as much as he loved it. He was ready to pare down to four. In 1999, after six years on the Ranch, the Macallisters headed north to San Mateo and came alongside a young church fellowship there. God's sovereignty again proved sweet.

First off, we moved into this funky/amazing house with a little stream running beneath it. (That was always the highlight we shared with others.) In a city with very little yard space anywhere, we lived the exception - on a veritable wood complete with deer and raccoon. It really was great, though soon-to-be-discovered, too dark for Mark's liking. Levi and Bree shared a room - because the third bedroom was w-a-a-a-y far away downstairs and down the hall.

Their spot was cute though. All divided up so they'd have their own space. Lots of windows. It felt like they were in a tree house. Actually we all felt like we were in a tree house.

When we first moved to the Bay Area, I homeschooled the kids for a while rather than put them somewhere midyear. We had quite the set up in our huge living room divided by free standing bookshelves, surrounded by more built-ins in one corner. That was our little niche with table and chairs and all our school supplies, a sweet season for me with the kids.

As fifth and third grades approached for Levi and Bree, respectively, I took a job with a private Christian school and the kids joined me there. It was great as it saved much in tuition money and provided a little help with living expenses - which are crazy in the Bay Area, by the way. It was also perfect in being able to keep school hours, vacation days, etc. I was thankful that the Lord allowed the perfect work scenario for the Macalllisters.

Mark was Assistant Pastor at the church and once again, became immersed in all the ins and outs of serving folks. Having been in ministry for many years, he was able to bring some elderly wisdom and was a much appreciated addition to the leadership team there. We loved that little church filled with genuine people who were committed to loving and serving the Body. And it was all great for a while…

But Mark didn't fare well. And because his depression surfaced some out of sync with his cycle, we saw a doctor or two only to be diagnosed with SAD - Seasonal Affective Disorder. Ugh.

*****

The doctor said many people moving to the Bay Area, likewise the rainy Northwest, did not handle or transition into the gloom and dreary of these similar climates. Why didn't we factor the meteorological conditions into our move-making decision? I can't tell you, but all of a sudden we felt pretty nervous about our relocation choice. I mean if people with no history of depression struggled here, how were we to survive?

We tried. Mark bought a light box from Sweden, - or was it Norway? He changed his diet to maximize every serotonin boosting possibility. He tried to be more disciplined in lifestyle in many ways - not his strong suit - but the effect was not great.

In hindsight, we probably were straddling a cycle. The lines blurred sometimes… Let's see, it seems our years fell hardest at '86, '91, '96, thus far, but the build up and recovery could stretch our seasons to 18 months or so. So, year 2000, yes, yes we were on the front end of a cycle as Mark, again, struggled to get out of bed - trying to maintain some normalcy. And then SAD. Really God?

*****

For my part, God had done something precious in me through our last bout of craziness (1996-97) and I was still basking in an easy access to His presence that I'd never known before. I've told folks in relaying my story, that I was born again, again (like thrice!) as a result of that most horrible season of my life. Somehow God did what He does best and redeemed devastation and made it beautiful. I was so in love with Jesus that I rode this Bay Area dive a little higher on the water. That's not to say it was easy, but I was in a different place, a more secure place than previous seasons.

And, as usual, there was a theme or focus to my God-fellowship again. This time it was *home* and in it was hope.

At some point, a guest speaker came to church and spoke about our home in the Lord and I began reading books on the topic and scouring scripture pertaining to home. The gist of my direction was twofold: 1) a citizenship in Heaven / eternal perspective, and 2) home in God Himself / He **IS** Home. My Faithful Father showed me over and over again that only in Him was I home - the home for which my heart truly longed.

In some sweet, more tangible ways, there were earthly applications too. Like the time when one of our pastors spoke a word over the Macs - "He's preparing a home for you - this isn't it." - Meaning, basically, that we hadn't found it yet. And the time when The Lord spoke to me saying - much as He did to King David - "because you have desired to build a home (in your heart) for Me, I will build a home for you." Ahhh, Sweet Lord, that revelation still causes tears.

*****

Mark did not hit rock bottom at this point. We were in more of a *muddy* season than black one and, in some ways Mark maintained well, rising up much like during our fire season. For a variety of reasons beyond just the SAD diagnosis, after 18 short months in the Bay Area, we Macallisters were again asking the Lord, "Where to now?" On some levels we were hugely saddened. As I said earlier, we loved our church and the tight community of friends. We also felt some grief over what we were putting Levi and Bree through, - another goodbye, and a tearing away from what had become familiar people and places. (We were boosted in the encouragement from God, however, that these challenges were prime opportunities to display His faithfulness to our children.) On some levels, we were excited. Since we felt we were obedient in moving north to Belmont and because it was obvious we couldn't stay there, we had a sense of God's hand paving our path. That's always a good place to be. What's He doing? Where are we going? It's gotta be good.

While the kids and I were winding things up at home, Mark took a little research trip. We had narrowed our move choices to three places: San Diego County; Cedar Crest, New Mexico; and somewhere near family in Colorado. Mark wandered San Diego but never made it to Colorado; Cedar Crest grabbed him first. And that was fine with me.

BACK TO NEW MEXICO

We got a phone call from Mark that he'd decided on New Mexico, that he'd put down a deposit on a rental home in the mountains, and that he was on his way home to load up the moving truck. It was a whirlwind, I tell ya.

One night before taking off we gathered a large group of friends at our home to say Thank You for their love and support. We spent some time in prayer and I remember the Lord saying the Macs were carrying the fragrance of Jesus with us in this move. That was sweet to me. I knew He went with us; I knew He'd be there when we arrived. But the nuance of this statement was personal and intimate to me. He was so near, His scent was on us. We smelled like Him. (I want that always.)

With sad and expectant hearts, family of four, one cat and a good friend crossed some of the ugliest terrain in the country (complete with overheating rental truck, etc) and two days later made it to Cedar Crest, New Mexico.

Home again, home again, jiggity jig. That's what it seemed like.

*****

Mark found us a wonderful house with living room, wall to wall and floor to ceiling, window panels overlooking our beautiful mountain. Right outside the windows was a wrap around porch and we spent lots of time both in the living room looking out and outdoors looking further. I have a visual of Levi and Bree in their sleeping bags on the floor near the windows and watching one of NM's famous lightening shows. We had fantastic storms and the outdoors created better entertainment than any TV movie.

We left California mid-summer so the kids could finish up their school year; when we got to NM one of our first orders-of-business was to determine where they'd attend next. And God was so good. We still weren't quite ready for public education so it was great to discover a Christian school about seven minutes from home (unless factoring in winter snow and then it could take awhile). Now we had the house thing down, and the kid thing. It was time to earn a living.

Feeling led back to New Mexico by the Holy Spirit, Mark and I were fairly confident that God would pave a path in this arena also. And what was on Mark's heart? Again. Full-time, U.S. missionary-style ministry to access-restricted countries in Asia. Mark's first ministry love was China going back to before I knew him and, over time, this focus broadened to encompass most of the East-Asia countries persecuted for faith in Jesus. After much prayer, we decided now - if ever- was the time to go for it and see if God would back a full-time pursuit of Asia ministry.

ASIA FRONTLINES

We had plenty of rooms in our house so Mark set up shop in one of them and got to work. Since 1983, Mark had maintained relationship with many folks we'd encountered on our various trips overseas; fortunately, this meant he really wasn't starting from scratch. He began setting a framework for partnering with our friends - both overseas and stateside - with lots of vision, but primarily with a humble heart desiring to come alongside those laboring to serve their own indigenous people. (I think this desire describes a part of Mark's gifting: serving the servants.) Another component of this deal was to raise our own support income, a rather uncomfortable thing to do as anyone who has been there knows. Fortunately, again, Mark's rapport with churches, ministries and people made this process a little easier. We were blessed over and over again by folks just wanting to be a part of what we were doing.

Bible couriering had morphed into pastoral and leadership training. Although getting precious Bibles into the hands of persecuted believers was still a priority of western Christians, God seemed to put a new direction on Mark's heart. Plus, if Mark were to get caught at the border a time or two (and he'd already been caught once back in 1984/85), ministry would end with his name blacklisted at all of Asia's borders. Couldn't have that if we were in for the long haul. Thus, Mark began developing teaching/training material to take overseas for the benefit of leaders gathered to learn and grow with very little accessible resources. We were privileged to work with many gifted, Jesus-loving men and women here in the States who felt equally privileged to export their learning to brothers and sisters in

81

access-restricted Asia. Some accompanied Mark and did their own training. Some went on their own with Mark's assistance in accommodating their travel, etc. Some just sent material with Mark. Whatever the case, Asia Frontlines planted seeds, watered them, pulled weeds, bore fruit and harvested it over the years - to the Glory of God.

*****

It was either Mark's first or second trip to Asia in his new role that was scheduled three weeks following September 11, 2001. Like most Americans, we walked in a fog for awhile following the unfathomable attack on our county. I think most people, to be honest, would say they got very introspective and reevaluated life on many levels. Besides agonizing over the loss of life and the plight of our county, we Macs wondered if travel to Asia was a good idea at the moment, if Americans would be targeted all over the globe, if the kids and I would be safe without Mark for three weeks. It was disconcerting. Yet ultimately, God led Mark to go as scheduled, and the decision was on par with other decisions Mark made through the years of overseas travel that endeared him to our Asian brothers and sisters. One time he got very sick on his way to connecting with a brother in China. At any other time he might have decided to check into a hotel and ride it out or, more likely, check into a hospital. But he knew people were counting on him and there was no real way to communicate delays or changes with such short notice. He showed up, and though he did need medical attention once he safely arrived, the family was deeply moved that someone would care that much for them to come and feel so rotten. We heard stories years later that Mark was known all over one particular region as the American Pastor who cared enough to show up when most others wouldn't have (or maybe didn't). Another time a brother in China went missing - fortunately not to prison, but due to communication issues he wasn't where he was supposed to be when Mark was heading to meet him. Rather than turn around and chalk this segment of connection off his itinerary, Mark began to pray that the Lord would allow him to find the contact. After two or three days and wandering a couple cities, Mark found his friend. His reputation continued to spread as the Pastor who cared, who was persistent and didn't give up in the face of challenges.

Over the course of the next five years, Mark averaged about two yearly trips overseas for three plus weeks each. In between he worked tirelessly serving Access-restricted Asia at home, building never a large, but solid, ministry geared towards equipping Asian leaders for their own ministries in their own countries. Mark highly valued communication and was good at keeping Asia Frontline's/ Mac family's supporters informed of all the highs and lows of working on behalf of the persecuted church.

And once again, "tirelessly" had good and bad connotations.

A "PRESSING THROUGH" SEASON

2001 actually would have been another marker year for Mark's cycle. And there were definitely tale-tell signs. I believe that much like the last season, Mark had lots of focus to keep him going. We moved in 2000. We started a ministry soon thereafter which Mark loved. Things on the home front and in vocation were new and required lots of time and attention and Mark rose to the occasion with excessive energy. Another factor was our decision to buy a house - our first ever after 17 years of marriage. We were vagabonds never landing anywhere long enough to consider planting, or, we lived in houses provided by our current ministries. Now, back in New Mexico, we were ready to stay.

Mark and I knew we wanted a home in the mountains we loved, and we spent several months wandering dirt roads and plotted communities looking for our dream. Funny thing, we ultimately found it within two or three blocks of our rental house just as the builder was adding the finishing touches to our sweet little 'New Mexico Ranch Style' home.

*****

So what did happen to that cycle? Well. It had been bobbing up for quite awhile but ultimately came again within months of our move. So, maybe a few months delayed but that hardly mattered, it still found a way. And it came with sleeplessness and anxiety and depression and, again, with anger. Recently Bree and I had a talk about the manifestations of pain, coming predominantly, either through sadness or anger. Wish I had more of an understanding of that in those mad days. I might have fared better.

I knew by now that we were in an abominable season. I knew that Mark was miserable. I knew that he could only minimally control his thoughts, behaviors, perspectives, etc. But, again, I thought maybe we'd skirt another episode. With each previous cycle, we had learned and grown, and I kept thinking/hoping that we'd never have to go back to the darkness. The first breakdown we found a med fix that made a huge difference. Great. No more breakdowns necessary. But, no. We were pummeled with other health issues that caused us to try other meds. Bad. But we learned not to do that again. So now we're good. But, no. Oh yeah; no more hospitalizations but almost a broken relationship. But we went to counseling and were restored. So now we're good. But, no. The anger back. I really didn't know if I could do this again.

The kids were older now and I was all about protecting them from the harsh reality of what was going on in and through Mark. I distanced myself from him just to avoid conflict and argument. Both were so petty and senseless. Unfortunately, I was goaded too often into the fray as I just could not stand it. My style was way more retreat and isolate and Mark could not stand that. I decided to go to counseling again and begged Mark to go with me; he thought me going was a good idea and that I should get my issues, my problems, straightened out. I was the one with problems; he didn't need to go. Grrrr...

But it was okay. I went and I benefited. And I connected with a wonderful woman who would be helpful years later, one more time.

It's funny, in a way, how much time I sorta wasted, though. Mark wanted me to go and not talk about him - only about me and my stuff. I honored that for awhile. Remember, I was the girl who looked forward to submitting to my husband. The day I mentioned Mark's cyclothymic condition to my counselor was a low point for me. I hated to disrespect Mark in doing so. Once out of my mouth, Rosalie looked at me astounded. "Honey. You can't separate your struggles and issues from that one. Don't you know? Mental illness affects everything and everyone in the family." Bam. A light bulb went on. Just like that.

*****

Per usual, God led me deeper into Him in my pain. I went through Mike Bickle's 24 week intensive study of the 'Song of Solomon' - one of the best things I've ever heard. All about God's amazing love for us - His bride. And I was starved for it. I spent a couple hours daily digging with Bickle into scripture and basking in Jesus' adoration of me. Incredible. (Every person with whom I've ever compared notes on this study has said it's life changing. Truly it was.)

We had a lovely front porch at our Cedar Crest home and I remember taking my Bible, notebook and CD player outside and sitting at the table there to study. Even as Jesus was pulling me closer and closer to Him, I still felt the irony of my circumstances. Here I was in the home of my dreams, with my tight little nuclear family - the prettiest of pictures to most outsiders - yet I was gasping inside, not sure if everything might totally crumble around me. I used to just ache when I'd see Levi and Bree, mostly oblivious (and glad they were) bounding towards me or Mark for hugs and connection. They didn't know how precarious their lives were at the moment. For the most part Mark managed to restrain his emotions around the kids. Once in a while, though, something stupid would happen. Like the time when He was working in our laundry room on the dryer. Something piqued him and he had a little rant going on. Levi finally said, "Dad. Why are you so mad?" That deal turned into a good thing as Mark pondered the question and worked harder at managing his outbursts. But that's the whole point, I guess. He had to work hard against an irrational mind and it was exhausting. He often knew he was out of control - as though from a distance - but felt totally unable to fix what was happening. For me, - I knew he was out of control, but I still wanted him to stop the madness and be *in* control. My head would swirl with endless questions: How much of this was manageable and if any part was, then what was it? And what should Mark be doing? And what should I be doing? And was it better for me to prod him towards it or to stay out of his way so he wouldn't be angry? Oh my gosh. I'm weary just dragging those thoughts out of dusty drawers.

*****

What Mark lost in normalcy, he made up for in hard work. All through this cycle, he pushed and pushed to further all the Asia projects stateside and overseas. Somehow God produced fruit regardless of Mark's mind. - Now why we thought we could just stay in ministry as though nothing was wrong, I can't tell ya. Kind of like our previous cycle at the Ranch; it was our life. I think Mark and I were both scared that without it, we would have nothing. I groan saying that even now.

On the other hand, maybe it was God's grace. A fellow pastor and friend, years ago, shared with Mark and me that if all ministry workers ditched out due to problems and trials in their lives, no one would be left to work the Kingdom. That was so helpful for me. I had shared with this friend that I felt so hypocritical; I was so messed up. Mark and I were so messed up. He hugged us, said he'd often felt the same and encouraged us to keep open to Jesus; to regularly confess our challenges, anxieties, and sins; and to love the Lord. We were okay. Kinda.

*****

Slowly, slowly we staggered out of another season. And as with our Ranch episode, there was not a clear indicator of the finish line. A gradual sense of stress reduction, not so much eggshell walking, and maybe a laugh here and there seeped into our days and we moved on. Unlike our Ranch episode, I don't recall Mark and I talking about the grand transition; we didn't counsel together this bout. Each cycle had its unique qualities and this one, though I called a *spade a spade* was not so accepted by Mark as such. Maybe in hindsight with a lot of thought he saw it this way, I'm not sure. But we didn't talk about it much. It was too exhausting. You know the things in life that have no answers? There are plenty of them. This cyclothymic deal had beaten us, in a sense, this time. As I said earlier, with each passing hellish season we thought we had things figured out; we thought we knew how to prevent another. But ruthlessly, they'd come again. And again. As much as I thought, "Stop: Let's implement A, B & C, now," I had no confidence that we could really do anything differently. Yet I was double-minded. A part of me wanted to take control and, at least, try the *perfect* scenario. But what was that? And I was far from being in control of anything. I could barely bite my tongue or abstain from reacting to hurt at times. Ahhh Lord. (Recently I heard Pastor James MacDonald answer the question: What do you regret in life? His reply: "My responses and reactions to hurt." Isn't that the truth? Me too.)

Something else that I didn't like much, but couldn't seem to help, was the toughened exterior that I'd built around me. My self-protection made me distant and borderline unfeeling. Or at least out of touch with my feelings. My counselors were in agreement that I was emotionally frozen. It was such a catch-22 because, when Mark was out-of-cycle, he needed to know me and felt he didn't sometimes because I was such a straight line: no highs or lows. Just flat. But I was less and less able to feel anything. It was survival mode. Oh how I wanted to survive. How I wanted the Macallister family to survive.

At the prompting of my past and present counselors, I threw a lot of glass dishes against the backside of our house. Occasionally the madness of my reality would prompt me to go outdoors and do such a crazy, non-Jody-like activity. I remember a few times the tears welling up and then exploding and I became a wet, soggy mess, - exhausted. But that was about the extent of any emotion in me; I had to work at it.

*****

Fortunately, in time and following this 2002ish cycle, life improved quite a bit. Mark and I recovered our grooves and enthusiastically moved forward.

I went back to work, full-time, doing something new. I became a school teacher. This seemed to make sense as Mark was doing Asia ministry, exclusively, and we were fully contributor supported. Though our needs were graciously covered by our Faithful Father, we wanted to be wise and future-planning. Plus, we had both kids in private (i.e. costly) school for a while now. With me teaching where they attended, the expense was more manageable. I think I only taught one year with Levi still there before he headed up the road to High School. I was with Bree for three. And, really, what fun it was to be able to work in the same building where my kids spent seven hours a day. Couldn't get much better than that for a mom who wanted to be hands on. Mark was pleased to have me with them as well. He felt better about me working, in general, due to the circumstances as he always wanted me to be a stay-at-home mom. He wanted to be that man who enabled his wife to do so and I cherished that.

So I had a busy life beyond working alongside Mark for the first time ever. And it was healthy for us. Maybe we weren't smart previously. Many folks had said it was rare for husband and wife to work jointly without killing each other and advised against it. Maybe we were stubborn. We'd met and fallen in love over our common heart for missions/Asia. We were in it together from Day One and it seemed right that we work at it hand in hand. And actually we did well a lot of the time outside of our unique seasons. All to say, for both Mark and myself, it was a bit of a sad departure yet we recognized the good in it, also. I think it was a healing season for us. We worked hard and we missed each other at the same time. We missed the companionship of a common ministry purpose, yet it wasn't so far removed and we grew more connected again emotionally even as we were more distant physically. Ahhh. Good thing God is Smart and Stubborn in His own right.

*****

I have a distinct memory of jogging down a beautiful dirt road on our mountain and thinking, "I love my husband." It was rejoice-worthy. That's where I was at in the moment, but sad to say, my heart didn't sing that tune often. Not that I didn't love Mark, I always did. But my heart didn't rejoice in that truth. It was hard. And the fact that it was hard made me incredibly sad. It shouldn't be that way. I wanted to rejoice. So when I was enabled, it was a giddy deal. I was so happy to be happy in love. Praise God for those times.

To elaborate on that note, I want to say Mark was a great man. When he wasn't plagued by darkness on one end of the continuum or the other, he was selfless. He'd do anything for anybody - most of all for me, for Levi, for Bree. He loved us in an I-don't-know-how-to-do-this way therefore he veered towards I'll do it/be it at my own expense. I ache to remember his eagerness and vulnerability in living like this. (Surely You formed his inward parts, Lord. Oh how You loved him.)

So when I say, "it was a giddy deal" in rejoicing about loving Mark, it's because life was hard more often than not. Not that Mark wasn't *love-worthy*. Simply: giddy was rare.

*****

Life circumstances evolved over the next few years. Mark continued pouring heart and soul into Asia ministry; I continued working, taking education college courses and doing the housewife/mom balancing act. Mark made his two trips yearly to visit our persecuted family overseas; I became involved in Women's Bible Studies and extra-curricular school activities. Levi and Bree were making us proud in school and in their pursuits of God-given talent. I was praising God that our family was seemingly healthy and was breathing a little less cautiously.

In 2005, after teaching three years at our God-send little Christian school, I resigned when Mark was asked to go back on Calvary's church staff to assist a new and younger pastor. This appeared God's timing and Mark welcomed the challenge of converging passions: local church and overseas missions. He so loved this church he helped to birth in the 80's and was excited about the opportunity before him to love it some more. As Mark was taking on more and would be in town (30 minutes from home) regularly, we thought it time for me to be home again - available to my, now two, high school kids. Though Levi had been establishing himself for a couple years at East Mountain's charter school, Bree was just starting and I didn't want to be bound by my job and inaccessible to them and the High School experience. I stepped back into a supportive role with the Asia ministry and began a new balancing act.

*****

There were challenges to this new look of our lives. There always are, yes? Some of them, honestly, are outside the personal parameters of this story. Others are contributing, however, like the very real and raw heartache Mark experienced regarding the all-too-public conflict taking place in and around his beloved Calvary Chapel in 2005/2006. Even in the healthiest of times, Mark didn't fare well with family dysfunction and disunity. (Who does?) Enough said.

Another five or six months. This is where I'm at, Mark. December: Advent Season.

Today the awesome message at church was on joy and how we can know Joy even when happiness isn't in the equation. That's a very personal message for me, for so many I know. It's been the bedrock of my life for several years now - maybe close to three decades. This Joy makes me groan and long for Home.

I had one of those glimpses into Heaven this morning while worshiping - even before the message and hearing its truth. Recalling an encouragement I offered a young friend who'd lost her dad months ago, I sensed the Lord showing me how close Heaven is. A book was opened and a page was turned. One page. That's it. The turning of a page. I then saw what appeared to be a TV stage with the facade of a house. The camera boom panned from one room to the next. The thinness of a wall. Two rooms, a door frame in between. That's it. Walking through the open door. Walking from one room to the next.

And it made me cry. It made me ache. I almost saw living on both pages, back-to-back, - living in both rooms, side-by-side. Earthbound and Heaven so close. So close. I saw the page turn and I sensed my hand reaching for the wall flattening against it. Touching the separation. Being so close.

You are not far off, Mark; you are near. On the next page, in the next room.

In The End

2006

It was early January and I was suffering from PVB's. (Everyone know that's Post Vacation Blues?) I was trying to look at the new year enthusiastically while out jogging the hard, winter packed, dirt roads of my mountain. It was a blustery, not very pretty morning and the wind was making me irritable, which it tends to do too often. I was disappointed; this was not the glistening, bright January weather I'd hoped for.

Slowly God somehow got my attention however, despite my negativity, told me He was with me, and turned my heart and gaze towards Him. All before clearly saying, "This is a year of blowing winds."

Oh God.

*****

2006. Yep. It was the 5th year again… 1986, 1991, 1996, 2001… Not precision clockwork, mind you, but clearly overarching… But maybe since the 2001 cycle hit harder in 2002, I heard wrong. Maybe my irritability was speaking. Satan, get behind me.

I got home and shook the seeming darts from my skin, captured my racing thoughts, hung a prayer and, per usual, distracted myself with the here and now. What could I do? Really. What else could I do?

*****

Levi was a Junior in High School, Bree a Freshman. Mark was

working at Calvary and doing a lot of activities with small groups while juggling Asia Frontlines ministry from home. I tried to give consistent part-time effort, as well, to maintain a full-time presence in our overseas endeavor. All to say, we were a busy household; life was never boring.

I settled into routine as the New Year got into full swing and began to relax some as Mark's biannual trip to Asia approached in February. This year he was taking along a beloved and favored partner… Levi. Mark and I had always wanted to get our family overseas, preferably all together, but that was a pretty pricey deal. We never could really afford to do that on our own and didn't feel comfortable asking our contributors to buck-up for a Macallister family outing. Ah well. Mark would take Levi this year and get Bree overseas two years down the road in her Junior year. Preparations were full steam ahead. Mark was fine; I had been fine until typical *mom nerves* set in at the thought of my child hopping on a plane and gallivanting across Asia. I mean I knew Mark. He would get busy and convey all kinds of confidence that Levi could fend for himself and Levi would be out on his own, and… Good thing I didn't know, at the time, how my concerns materialized. Only later did I learn that Levi *did* wander out in Bangkok - and who knows where else - on his own while Mark was in meetings. Needless to say, I prayed a lot while my boys were gone and God faithfully brought them home with many a tale to tell.

*****

In New Mexico, the school year starts mid August and gets out mid May. Seems Mark and Levi were just barely home and, zoooooom, school was out for the summer. And sometime in that season, Mark began to have back problems.

I shouldn't really say began. Mark had sporadic back pain for as long as I'd known him. I remember one night before we were married back in my parent's house, he lay on the floor and writhed in agony, his back spasming uncontrollably. After 10 minutes or so it stopped as quickly as it'd begun and that was the end of it - at least to that extreme - for a long time. Kinda freaked me out. I felt so helpless.

Apparently, Mark had a construction injury before I knew him.

I don't believe he had x-rays or any other imaging done. He just laid low a while, rested, and then was back to work when he felt better. Youth. When the Macs were living in the Bay Area, Mark had a nasty fall running to first base at a church softball game. It still makes me cringe to remember. He was running full speed when the first baseman bent over in front of him and Mark flipped over the guy's back and landed on his own hip/back. I could hear the thud in the bleachers and thought surely he'd broken something. A teammate took him to the hospital, but again, the injury was minimized and Mark came home to recoup for a few days, took plenty of painkillers and kept going.

Over the years, though, there were several times when back spasms would hit or Mark would experience lower back pain. Progressively he got to the point where he didn't like long drives because they were painful sitting so long and we, sadly, avoided most road trips. The long flights overseas were also pretty hard on Mark. I'm sure he was one of those passengers you'd often see walking the aisles.

Although he attempted exercise, stretching, dieting and chiropractic over the years, nothing seemed to really be long lasting for some reason or another. And many things would trigger a pain episode. Mark was never one to shy from hard manual work, or to sit for hours on end working in front of a computer screen, - both to his detriment. He was an *all in* kind of guy and not one to quit before a job was done no matter how taxing.

I don't recall if there was a specific pain trigger or not in 2006. Likely it was an accumulation of many things over the years but one day Mark dropped to the floor and couldn't move. Levi had friends over and I remember them carrying Mark out to the living room where, though in pain, he had plenty of floor space to spread out. We hoped some down time and rest would do the trick but things were never quite the same from that point on.

WINDS

I'd always heard of people's backs going out and figured that's what had happened to Mark. This deal was obviously a bigger one than past back episodes, but I wasn't overly concerned. This was a tangible problem; tangibles had fixes and we'd be on the other side of this one in no time. Mark slowed down some and did try to implement a healthier lifestyle when it came to working, resting and eating. We thought maybe shedding a few pounds would be good, and paying workers to do the heavy projects, and going to bed at a decent hour. And exercise and stretching were good. And a multitude of home remedies should be good. But the *wind* kept blowing; ultimately, there wasn't enough relief and we ended up seeking the expertise of physical therapists, chiropractors, acupuncturists and orthopedists. Ugh.

Per Mark's MRI, he had a herniated disc. Simple. Doctors from San Francisco to Stanford to New Mexico chimed in and all recommended surgery to correct his back problem. Around that same time, we knew two guys Mark's age who had the recommended surgery and were up and about the next day and back to routine within a week's time. Seemed the smart route to take.

We didn't move on a date that quickly, however, because Mark was up and down. Some days the pain was hardly noticeable and we'd think things were improving. There was a long stretch of manageable discomfort early fall and though I can hardly imagine it now, Mark even went to Asia for his biannual trip late October. I remember contemplating the wisdom of that trip, but overall, as Mark did seem to be holding his own, we thought he should go. Our Asian friends were counting on him.

*****

Though I don't believe there was anything, specifically, about that trip that set Mark over the edge, I do think it was hard on him generally speaking. He did a lot of traveling in far reached areas of Burma where roads were poor and weather rutted. Imagine vehicles from the 60's and 70's and you might envision some of his journeying. As usual, Mark was on several planes and slept on a variety of surfaces ranging from the overly soft to the concrete floor. So what was not worth mentioning for a healthy, young guy became a little more noteworthy to my, then, 53 year old husband. He came home pretty darn sore.

And he could no longer get comfortable. The recliner that previously provided the best position didn't any more. None of our beds seemed to work so a mat on the floor was the answer for sleep, - what Mark could get of it, that is. Sleep became more scarce and that was another problem.

So we did, then, decide on a surgery date: December 26, the day after Christmas, 2006.

*****

Snow was predicted for Christmas night and though I hated to do it, Mark and I headed for town that evening leaving Bree home alone. Levi was in town with his girlfriend. Both kids would be fine, but I didn't like us all scattered on Christmas. It felt sad and lonely. On the other hand, Mark had been experiencing increasing pain and weariness and I was a bit frazzled myself. It seemed best to get to town, stay overnight with a friend (thus mitigating snow delays) and get to the hospital at the crack of dawn for a 7:30 surgery.

Sure enough, we got to Albuquerque and the snow started. We were thankful for our gracious host who set us up in a beautiful guest room and after some brief fellowship, Mark and I turned in for the night. Mark was in too much pain to sleep in the bed with me so we had a futon mattress on the ground. We talked a while and as I turned out the lights, "Jody?"

"Hmmm?"

"If anything happens to me during surgery tomorrow and I don't make it, I love you."

"You'll make it, Mark. You'll make it."

*****

We awoke to one of New Mexico's record snowfalls. Talk about *wind* challenges. I never did become a great, confident winter driver and our friend offered to follow us to the hospital to make sure we got there okay. We allowed extra driving time for unplowed roads and did manage to make it to surgery on time. Both Mark and I were somewhat nervous but oh so hopeful that today would bring an end to the back pain that pretty much shut down normal living. I sat in the waiting room, prayed and observed others waiting with me. It's always kinda trippy being in those situations, wondering what life story is sitting in the next chair and the next. There's a lot of camaraderie in those types of places.

About 90 minutes after saying goodbye to Mark, his doctor came strolling out to let me know surgery was over and everything was fine; took care of that herniation, no problems. Within another 30 minutes, I was in recovery at Mark's bedside as he roused from the anesthesia. Nurses came and went and kept checking Mark's comfort level which, unfortunately, never seemed to register. Mark was in pain from the get-go. And the nurses were anxious to get him up and moving and out of the hospital so they were a little impatient with him. Not good. He kept telling them he wasn't feeling better at all, but ultimately, it was time to go (insurance rules). We walked gingerly out the doors with a small stash of pain pills and some sketchy post surgical instructions.

A friend from the mountains came and met us so we could get home. His car was more conducive to transporting Mark, and more able to handle the snowy roads some of which were still not plowed. I slowly followed Mark and Steve in our 4-wheel-drive the 20 miles to Cedar Crest, then left our car at the local grocery store. Steve got us the rest of the way to our doorstep and it was tense. Mark was bracing at every bump and turn, wincing with every move and breath.

Oh dear God; c'mon drugs. Start working.

It was good to get home, but as one hour after another came and went with no pain relief, Mark and I began to panic some. We called the hospital and yet another friend who worked with spine doctors. The hospital said such things as, "Sometimes it takes awhile." Our friend said, "They never should have let you leave the hospital while still in pain." - Great. We're 20 miles from the hospital. It's almost dark by now. Roads are icy and snow packed. Our car is a 15 minute hike away. We were going nowhere.

Also by this time, I was trashed. Physically, mentally, emotionally trashed. I started feeling feverish and knew I had to get to bed. Maybe if Mark took another little pill he could sleep and we could put this "terrible, horrible, no good, very bad day" to rest. (Thank you, Judith Viorst, for the perfect description.)

*****

Mark was sleeping in Levi's room (since Levi was still in town) and sometime in the night he called out to me. He was cold and in pain. In my own semi-delirium, I roused enough to walk across the house and throw another blanket on Mark, but that wasn't *compassionate*. And my actions were a note of contention in what became yet another season from hell: Cycle #5, just beyond the *blowing winds* of 2006.

CAN IT GET ANY WORSE?

The next day was really no better. Mark was still in significant to excruciating pain and we were on the phone as soon as doctors' offices opened hoping for a quick fix. Maybe someone overlooked something. Maybe a nurse forgot a key med for the post op cocktail. Maybe the doctor skipped a line on discharge instructions and an ice pack would take care of everything. We needed some relief quick. -- Although my brain would not allow for worst case scenario, although I kept trusting it was just a matter of time until we were on the right side of surgery, nothing seemed to get better. There might have been a tiny bit of reprieve now and then immediately following med intake, but it never lasted the four to six hours as indicated.

Per usual in the cycle years, I never really knew what came first: the chicken or the egg so I was always in this hazy realm of not knowing what to do. This season was no different and was way beyond my understanding. But anyone who has experienced painkillers, either personally or via a family member, knows they're bad news. I got that through my head quickly but, - were we experiencing a cycle on top of pain meds or, was this all about a back surgery gone bad and drugs making it worse? I doubt if there was a person on the planet able to answer that question.

Mark was convinced, as were a couple physical therapists we saw on yet another quest for wellness, that his surgeon nicked a spinal nerve. They told us *it happens,* and surgeons don't admit to it, but the distress should decrease with time as the nerve slowly heals. For now, Mark was in tears daily as needle-like spasms shot viciously and sporadically through him. Beyond that, the torment was constant.

Often, when Mark could hardly breathe for the pain, he'd run outdoors and hang on this old jungle gym that some family next door left behind years ago. He'd grab the metal bars, lift his feet from the ground and somehow there'd be the slightest relief - from his vertebrae stretching, I suppose. I used to follow him many times and stand near him and cry, myself, as his tears dripped to the ground. It was absolute agony.

*****

So this time we weren't looking for answers to depression and anxiety and anger, but maybe we should have been. These things were building behind the pain front. Nope; this time we sought more chiropractors, physical therapists, massage, decompression and pain specialists, holistic physicians and multiple surgeons. We had more x-rays, MRI's and CT scans - all inconclusive. No one could determine absolutely what was going on but everyone had an opinion, of course. And we were desperate. Once again, we tried every suggestion presented and Mark was a guinea pig one more time.

Being that our doctors were miles away in town, we found ourselves driving from Cedar Crest into Albuquerque often. For most folks this was a pleasant jaunt and totally a worthwhile time expenditure to be able to live in the mountains. But when you can't sit for escalating pain, our health endeavors seemed self defeating. We couldn't catch a break for anything. And the elusive *search for a fix* was wearing us thin. At some point we slowed our breakneck pace with medical/health appointments and prayed the meds would sustain some semblance of relief.

What we didn't know - or maybe it was just me who didn't know - was that the pain meds were causing their own kind of craziness. Mark's sleep patterns became more and more irregular, thus anxiety building, and that ol' anger nemesis started raising its ugly head again. It actually peeked out that first night after surgery, as I already mentioned, but I had no idea how big a face it could take on under the *influence* of pain meds. I was pretty naive about a lot of things.

*****

The fact that I blew in and out of the bedroom and quickly threw a blanket over Mark that first agony-filled, post surgery night seemed to fester in Mark. It was almost an obsessive thing with him. As his thinking became more and more convoluted with the meds, he repeatedly reminded me of my self-absorption and lack of love and caring. I was a terrible wife and person and a hypocritical Christian. Wow. Can't say I did too well with all those labels. On one level, I knew Mark was not in his right mind. We'd been here before. On another level, this anger exceeded anything I'd ever seen previously and my mind wrestled, again, with truth vs fiction in our reality. (How sinful was I? Maybe I really was just a self-righteous prig thinking only of myself and my comfort. Maybe I did only love myself.) Praise God I called a friend and mentor, a man who did know (due to his own experience) and he patiently explained to me what was going on, saying ultimately, "Jody, even if you were Mother Theresa or even Jesus, Himself, standing before Mark right now, he'd still be - irrationally - madder than hell. That's what pain meds do to a person." I couldn't exactly say, *Oh Happy Day,* but I was greatly relieved that this new insanity had a source and perhaps an end once we got past the pain.

Easier said than done and I won't go into all the horror stories. There were plenty of them, I can tell you. At some point, though, maybe in 2008 after a year of, will we survive? - Mark surfaced enough to say for himself: "I've got to get off these drugs." And he started trying.

A SLIGHT REPRIEVE

So after a year of blowing winds with all the initial back challenges, and a year of intense pain and drug craziness, things finally settled just a bit- somewhere mid 2008. Not greatly, mind you. Mark still was not pain free; he was still sleeping uncomfortably and restlessly on the floor every night, still not able to sit in a chair or in the car for over 10 to 15 minutes a stretch. But there were a few things that seemed to help some and that screaming, vicious pain no longer randomly attacked several times daily. End of cycle? Who knows?

I had some trouble rolling out of the intensity of 2007+. On the one hand God, once again, drew me close to His heart through a Biblical word study on peace. I worked through Strong's Concordance and dissected and digested every verse in the Bible containing this life-sustaining word and I was actually still working through it come 2008. I can do this amazing project little justice now, but suffice it to say: God came near. When all around me there was an unspeakable lack of peace, inside in the quiet and lonely places of my heart, I knew Peace. (It was incredible and I'm thankful the fruit of that season has carried me miles and miles down the road, yes even to this day.)

But my trouble was kind of like when you over exercise and run too far or lift too much. Figuratively, I felt wobbly with noodles for arms and legs. After holding up, being strong for a long time, I wanted to lie down and hibernate a while. But it was not to be. Sometime during 2007, Mark had given up his job at Calvary. Though the church was gracious and said they'd keep an open door for Mark returning, Mark didn't feel right about leaving a gap in the staff or the ministry, thus he resigned. And for quite some time beyond his resignation, we continued to be supported by Calvary, but at some point, towards the end of 2008, with no real return to health and the economy diving like it did, we were on our own again financially speaking. Our Asia ministry partners had faithfully sustained us to a significant degree through all our years of ups and downs, but recently many within had also been hit hard by individual job losses or church tithing decreases so the trickle down was felt in our home. Time for me to get another job.

*****

Levi had graduated from High School in 2007, was attending UNM (then not), and living in town so he was hardly home anymore. Bree was busy doing High School, had a job and she wasn't at home much anymore either. Guess it was a good time for me to go back to work. I was willing, but like I said, I was a bit wobbly and it took another push for me to get out there and do the job hunt thing. And as much as Mark felt it was the needful thing to do, I think it was really hard on him to have me join the workforce. - When Mark wasn't in the throes of darkness, he battled really disliking himself for all he put his family through. Me going back to work under these circumstances was just one more blot on his already messy life photo.

Makes me sad, because as difficult as it was in some ways, it was also very good for me. I was stretched outside of my comfort zone, yet Faithful Father met me and spoke out of Isaiah 42, telling me He was again leading me by the hand. .. along ways I did not know.

A good chunk of 2008 was spent finding our land legs after riding the cyclothymic storm, and forging ahead with what we hoped was not our new normal: chronic pain and a survival mode that left a lot to be desired in the quality-of-life department. Though things were better than 2007, things were not good. We didn't get the bounce into a fluid and busy life as following previous cycles. The back pain prevented that. A very common visual at our house was Mark standing at the breakfast bar, - computer, books, letters or whatever, spread all over the counter and the table behind him, - working as long as he could stand, then heading to the living room floor to ice his back and lay flat awhile. Actually, at some point, he got a back support belt and packed ice underneath it so he could be freezing 24/7. Ice was the only help and though it didn't totally do away with the pain, it kept it at bay. That was something.

Because Mark did have an occasional decent day here and there, we were back to searching for health and wellness. (I say that as though the hunt ever completely stopped. It didn't. Sometimes we were just more highly motivated and able than others to do the homework, then actually get in the car and do the face-time with doctors, procedures, tests and hamster wheels.) Sometimes we would get our hopes up. Mark would experience a measure of relief and we'd think we were on to something only to plateau or downward spiral after some brief respite. This very process, I sometimes think in hindsight, was more demoralizing than it was worth. But in the moment, you do what you have to do; we had to try. We had to find a way out of our mess…

*****

A picture I can't seem to shake right now - so guess I better commit it to paper - is of Mark laying for hours and days on end in Levi's room. Over the course of four years, I can't even tell you how many hours he spent in that bed. Because Mark was a bad sleeper to begin with and then because of a bad back and persistent pain that prevented comfort in any one position for long, he started sleeping in what became the spare bedroom. It was mostly so I could have some night continuity and not crash and burn myself. - The picture in my head is almost a spinning one: the seasons changing from one to the next outside Levi's window as Mark lay in that room. I'm spanning several years, and jumping ahead, also, to present the full picture, but it's such a representative visual of what Mark's final years looked like. Before I got my job, and after (because I was part time), I would go lay next to Mark on the bed and we'd look out the window and talk and hope together. There was a tree right outside and big sky beyond; we'd note the sunny days and the windy ones, the rainy ones and the snowy ones. For a couple sweet seasons we spent many days watching a mama bird fly back and forth to her nest feeding her babies. She was so faithful; her young ones so needy. God provided; He cared for these insignificants. Surely He cared for us.

*****

111

Another scene I've recalled in my mind's eye recently is that of an Easter gathering with our friends in our home - probably in 2008 or 2009. Mark and I were privileged to do life with three special couples up in the East Mountains of New Mexico. We didn't hang out all the time and our connections got more sporadic with the Macallister challenges, but it was a - *for better or for worse* -priority to be together sometimes. Over the years, we created some great memories and our prayer gatherings were some of the best.

This Easter we did a foot washing. Our tradition was to do some sharing, praying and communion together, but this year we added the example of Jesus and each washed the feet of his or her spouse. It was sweet. And it was poignant. Mark, in all our current gatherings, lay on the floor in the middle of the room and this night was no different. We were quite a sight all squeezed into our living room, some sitting some kneeling, Mark in the middle, many of us weeping. Dang. The presence of Jesus is amazing.

WEARY

I'm honestly having a hard time remembering many details in this stretch of time. I know we had some life lines, such as friend gatherings, thrown our way. We even hosted a little Friday night prayer meeting with some other beloved folks so as to not become totally isolated on our mountain. Plus we needed the prayer desperately, ourselves.

As I mentioned earlier, Mark was never really the same following his back surgery. Preceding it, when his back went out, we were hopeful that it would be made right by operating. But it never was. There were small stretches of time - a week or two at the most - when things started looking up and we'd think, FINALLY. But they didn't last. And even though we survived the drug-crazy 2007 (which seemed the worst thus far), Mark was slowly but surely spiraling deeper and deeper into depression - shooting any mid-cycle, real reprieve, to hell.

*****

I started reading lots of books and online articles regarding pain, depression and the combination of the two. Not a good combo, but oh so prevalent. Very interesting, too, if it weren't for the loathing I had for the topic. . . . depression creating phantom pain, spinal nerve and pain routes, neurosensors and transmitters grooved to continue precedent pain. I was also seeing, because of my job at a radiology and imaging center, countless people battling the whole pain-depression deal. I knew we weren't alone. I also knew Mark had a huge propensity to a larger darkness, one that had nothing to do with physical pain. I couldn't let my mind travel too far down that road.

For over 20 years now, I had not researched our scenario of cyclothymic mental illness. We were either dealing with it in such an *up close and personal way* and fighting for sanity and/or survival; or, I was running as fast and furious as possible away from the whole ordeal once our season passed. (By then I didn't want to think about making sense of any of it as though I could.) But this go I bought books - not just on pain perspectives mentioned above, but very specifically on depression and bipolar illnesses. And I learned so much, things that might have helped earlier had I known. One book in particular, was extremely encouraging in a weird sort of way, <u>A New Light on Depression: Help, Hope, and Answers for the Depressed and Those Who Love Them</u>, by David B. Biebel. This book was actually written by a psychiatrist and a pastor, both of whom had personal insight into depression. This was what I needed: medical and spiritual experts speaking to the causes, symptoms, vices, clinicals, etc, of what we were living.

In our fifth cycle, in 2006-2007ish, mental illness had not quite the stigma of our earlier years; but I tell you, it still wasn't easy. Many know that battling depression, let alone other psychiatric labels, is not necessarily *church friendly*. To add some grace here I will say, I think a lot of it is due to a lack of experience, understanding and education. Most people just don't know how to respond to the mentally ill or to persevere with them for the long haul. It's tough. It's plain unacceptable to some. And to medicate for head stuff? Wait just a minute. (I have to be careful here.)

Many, if not most people, never knew, right up to the end, how much Mark struggled. He was not opposed to speaking openly about his battles to those who needed to hear of them, to those who needed an identifying voice in their lives. But otherwise his illness was not a public offering. It was too touchy. Too uncomfortable (more for others than ourselves). Too speculative. Too divisive even. Too many opinions out there. Too many Job's Comforters. Mental illness is lonely.

But backspace to my learning... I was comforted to discover

common ground between many stories and depictions of those chemically or mentally challenged with our story. I realized that over years, the enemy of our souls did what he does best. He accused and condemned and twisted our hellish seasons into interpreting them as deserved justification, - for sins and behaviors and actions, and any number of things. Now don't get me wrong. I'm a firm believer in, you *reap what you sow,* and Mark was sinful like the rest of us. But to the extent that the enemy had a heyday magnifying Mark's *guilt*... Well, Mark was robbed. That's all I can say. And what I'm getting at is I learned that all the depression manifestations exhibited in Mark were pretty common. Even for the believer. Yes. Even for the believer. - Thank you for letting me discover that, Lord.

*****

I didn't have the energy to ponder much beyond my own front door at that time, but God did lead a few folks our way - even in the thick of things - for us to love and pray for in their own mental battles. Funny how that helped some. Helped Mark to rally a strength which he imparted to those Jesus loved.

HANGING ON & MILESTONES

Mark and I were regularly seeing a counselor - that wonderful woman I mentioned a few chapters back - and Mark's psychiatrist. We were praying with friends, had loads of people praying for us and were listening to various teachings online to stay connected with the church and be fed God's Word by those more carefree and able-to-focus than ourselves. To a small degree, Mark continued searching for medical answers to his back pain and looked into specialty clinics, non-traditional treatments and international options. For the most part these days, he lay on the floor with this very computer I'm using now, propped against his knees, and poured into Asia. Always Asia, always a heart for Asia.

And I'm glad for that. I'm glad he had something to nurture, something that kept him going so often. I'm hugely grateful, as well, for our beloved brethren across the ocean that held him up to the Father in prayer.

*****

I turned 50 in 2009. Even though I wasn't all that excited about being so *old* - I had envisioned celebrating in some fun way, years earlier, when life was easier. Now as the date approached, I just felt sad. I knew Mark wanted my big day to be special for me. He'd attempted a few grand ideas and actually he pulled off a really nice time for me with my three special East Mountain girlfriends. But he wasn't a part of any of it. He was at home on the floor.

Bree graduated from High School in 2009. Mark barely made it to Levi's graduation ceremonies in 2007 what for back pain. This year was about the same. He went; he rallied. But it was difficult. I remember at Levi's event, Mark sat and he paid for it after. At Bree's, he stood the entire time. Nevertheless, I'm glad he made it.

Our 25th Wedding Anniversary was also in 2009 and you know what? We experienced a brief reprieve around that time and enjoyed a little impromptu surprise party thrown on our behalf by sweet friends. Though, again, I had grander dreams for #25 years earlier, I was thankful Mark was up for any kind of celebrating at all. And thankful we had a 25th Anniversary. There was many a day I didn't think we'd last 25 years...

*****

Due to all the inflow/outflow of trial pain treatments and drugs, Mark's poor body was spent. When you're in the middle of desperately needing some relief, you'll try about anything. When it doesn't work, and in the aftermath, you second guess and wish you'd never gone *there*. Such a catch-22. As more days turned into weeks and months, it was clear Mark was in no way improving. He'd have some decent days here and there and we'd try to maximize and appreciate them, but for the most part, the pain still nagged, the depression still lurked. In years past, when cycles would strike, we'd adjust Mark's primary med, the MAO Inhibitor, and there would be some response, even if just a little recognition that it mattered. That wasn't the case now. And daily Mark began to verbalize the words I came to deplore, "I can't go on like this."

GOD OR A BRIGHT IDEA?

Ups and downs, hills and valleys, we trudged through them all. At some point, however, with much counsel, discussion and prayer, our only hope and option seemed to be to wean off what was now our 25 year crutch. Nardil. According to Mark's psychiatrist and common medical consensus, medicines often run their course and sometimes are rendered ineffective by nature of their long intake. The drug was obviously not helping Mark any longer, thus it seemed pointless to continue with it. Surely, after 25 years, there was something else out there that could benefit Mark's depression and cyclothymic condition. The doctor thought so. And really, we had nothing to lose at this point. Mark was not living.

But this was my nightmare. We'd always said we'd never go off the Nardil again. Yes, our reasons were different from our attempt 20 years ago, - substantive, - but not appealing in the least. Still, there was no reason to continue on the Nardil. Mark lay in bed or on a floor somewhere in pain and depression. Plus, if I haven't said it already, the Nardil was so contraindicative that many a potential pain reliever was ruled out for reasons of possible stroke or, yes, even death. What was once a life-giving silver bullet was now our nemesis.

So as I said, after much pursuit for wisdom, Mark and I finally decided the time had come to make a drastic change. In fear and trembling, we set the stage.

*****

119

We knew we couldn't do this deal alone. The time had come to really bare all and ask for help from family, friends and those who loved us. And it couldn't be haphazard. We needed committed prayer and intercession on a regular basis to see us through. I had this vision for two or three folks to be lifting Mark up daily and encouraging him via a phone call, text or letter. (Many of you reading now were likely a part of that great feat. Thank you for stepping up to the plate.)

I made a 31 day calendar with the initials of three or four persons covering each day and asked everyone to commit to one 24 hour prayer period a month for Mark - however that might look for him or her. I knew God would speak to our friends and instruct them in intercession. I was totally confident of this. As a matter of fact, my hope began to rise with this endeavor. I was filled with an expectancy that God had a plan for many in this Macallister battle, that it wasn't all about us at all. And over the months, I believe the testimonies of many would confirm this.

And April 2010, we began a final journey of sorts.

*****

I remember going to a Beth Moore international simulcast that April in Albuquerque with Bree and my special girlfriends. I'm not sure how that was pulled off, but there were women around the globe sitting in churches or venues in every time zone at exactly the same moment and, once again, I experienced a little taste of Heaven. The message was great but it was the worship that can still bring a lump to my throat as I recall singing with hundreds of thousands of women all at the same time from all over the world. Of course I couldn't hear the full impact, but I was very aware as the Holy Spirit quickened my senses, that I was praising my Savior with eternal sisters and that this was, indeed, just a taste of something unimaginable to come. Amazing. Absolutely amazing. And, oh, how I needed this timely perspective.

*****

Unlike in 1991, there were some medications out in 2010 that helped minimize withdrawals from the Nardil. That was hopeful. They were expensive, way expensive and not insurance covered, but we couldn't put a price tag on successively getting through the weaning. Once we finally made the decision to do this thing and got all our ducks in a row, as far as prayer coverage, etc, - things started looking up some. Mark and I planned our days around healthy activity, eating and resting and it felt good to be so intentional in the right direction. With the help of the interventional drugs, we were hopeful that with slow momentum, coming off the Nardil might actually be easier than anticipated.

I was still working part time so Mark and I would have our mornings together. Most days I'd get him some protein-rich breakfast and then we'd go for a walk around the roads of our neighborhood. We often moved like two very old people, holding hands, stopping to rest and enjoy our beautiful meadow or the views overlooking the mountainous valleys around our home. Fresh air. Sunshine. Deep breathing. God in our midst. I felt Him; I knew He walked with us.

And true to instruction, throughout those days, Mark would often have a voicemail, email or text awaiting him on our return. Oh the encouragement those words would bring. I felt so much better leaving Mark each afternoon for a few hours knowing he wasn't alone and that precious ones were continuing to carry him throughout his day in my absence. (To be absolutely honest, some days we didn't hear from anyone, but those were the exceptions and God always seemed to present Himself, somehow, in those times.)

Many days in this initial weaning season, despite the chronic back pain, I would come home from work and Mark would have dinner ready for us. Wow. What a treat. He was giving it his all and so wanted to contribute to the wellness efforts to which we were committed.

If we weren't so vulnerable, so fragile, I would describe this window of time as a happy one. In many ways, Mark was a better man - right now - than ever before. I'm not sure I can say why, but this evident *goodness* in him lasted the rest of his days - no matter how horrible things later became. I was glad for this display of a man then; I'm glad for it now. It's a treasure to me, a gift from Jesus.

*****

So again. We had our ups and downs. Somewhere in this med

121

weaning process we managed some heart-to-heart talks with Levi and Bree. As I said earlier, when the kids were younger I did everything possible to shield them from Mark's depression and subsequent cycles. By this age, that was no longer possible of course, and hadn't been for a few years. Nevertheless, they didn't have the big picture and now I was concerned with how they were processing their family realities.

Levi still wasn't around much. He was touring and doing his spoken word poetry. He'd also announced his engagement to Brandi Garcia so there were plans afoot to keep him occupied. Bree tried not to be home too often; I tried to be okay with that. This was a hard season for her what with her dad a mess. Mark's crazy drug year almost destroyed Bree's relationship with him. Those two were so alike in their strong wills and attitudes that they butted heads often, even in okay times. But with Mark in pain or med-influenced, it was particularly difficult. As the wife/mom caught in the middle, it was not fun to say the least. Even past that year, Bree struggled to accept Mark's *handicap* and I couldn't blame her. She just wanted a *normal* dad and family.

Our talks with the kids slowly unraveled Mark's past: from his depression-laden, bi-polar family tree, to his ingestion of a now noted "dangerous" anti-seizure medication prescribed at age 12 due to diagnosed epileptic activity in the family. He chose to quit taking that drug at age 18 and that was likely a smart decision. There was alcoholism in his family; Mark's mom had a brain tumor, benign yet problematic with coinciding hospitalizations and meds. And that's all the genetic foundation. Then there's the environmental. Mark's parents divorced when he was 12; a new man came on the scene shortly after; dad was typically absent and negligent wrapped up in a new woman; mom was present but emotionally negligent wrapped up in her new man; brothers were gone from the home old enough to be living their own lives. Mark lost in a fragmented, broken family (without Jesus until 18 or so). A perfect storm in so many ways.

These were the things we bared in much greater detail to our kids. Painful, painful things and, yet, I thought then and I think now what a perfect example of God's strength perfected in weakness. Mark was plenty broken, and plenty weak. But God did amazing things in and through Mark over the years. I mean seriously. All the opportunities Mark had to be a vessel of God's glory still just blows me away. - And we tried to raise this reality above all others before Levi and Bree. Yes, Dad had many counts against him as a child and young man. Yes, they colored his world and shaped who he was. Yes, he made mistakes and was a sinner just like everyone; his past didn't excuse everything. Yes, he unfortunately battled the inherent problems of his family of origin. BUT. LOOK WHAT GOD DID. Rescued him. Saved him. Called him into full-time ministry and missions. Allowed him new life, new family and an eternal home. That meant something.

It didn't fix everything, but it meant something. And something GOOD.

THE LAST ONE

I remember one day when I wasn't working - must have been summer because it was hot out - that Mark and I did a little day trip. Whenever Mark was up to it at all we'd try to get out; most of the time he felt like the walls were closing in on him which made sense being so isolated and home-bound. We took Timber, our boxer, and drove north a ways out past Madrid on Hwy 14 towards Santa Fe. It was beautiful out. Can't say enough about how gorgeous New Mexico is on some of its back roads. There's an old cemetery we tromped through for about an hour, careful not to step on broken headstones or mementos left from ages past. We read names and memories, sadness and joy on those plaques and crosses. Timber tore around chasing lizards offsetting any chance of somber. This cemetery was old, maybe not forgotten actually, but historic. No one had been buried there for decades. There was no grass, no trees, just dry brown vegetation giving it the appearance of abandonment. Mark and I really weren't somber, but there was something sacred about wandering this hallowed ground. We were very aware of the brevity of man, - a puff, a breath in time. We wondered the stories: entire families, multiple generations buried side by side; the mother and her newborn babe - date of death: one and the same; the young man: veteran of war; the beloved family pet alongside his master. I guess the mind blower in it all - and the discussion Mark and I had: God knew every single detail about every single one of those people down to the very number of hairs on their earth-living heads. And that was just one little cemetery in one little corner of the world in one little age of existence... And then, - Oh God. What is man that You are mindful of him?

Mark and I felt like we were alone on the planet, out there in the middle of nowhere, at some surreal cemetery, until along came another car, and a couple people and another dog. We headed back to Madrid and had a wonderful mid afternoon meal, sitting outside in one of the funkier towns in America. Another treasured memory. I remember Mark posting something on Facebook (before I ever hopped on), something simple like, "Today I get to take my wife on an outing." Ahhh. Praise God for that. Yep. We had a day like that here and there.

*****

Overall, Mark wasn't faring well. The less Nardil in his system the more depressed he got, even though, for the past two plus years, there was no recognizable benefit from the drug anyway. Innumerable times I heard the words, "I can't go on like this" and, "I'm not gonna make it." So many times my teeth were set on edge. STOP SAYING THAT. I can't hear that anymore. (I had my battles to fight, too.)

There was one treatment recommended years back that we had not yet tried, a chelation, non-AMA alternative in Baja California. The program had great results for cancer patients and many others battling a variety of challenging diagnoses. At the end of our rope, we finally decided to give this deal a try and Mark flew off to Baja for a couple weeks, - hoping against hope.

It was a rigorous, transfusion-like treatment with enriched fluids flushed through his system taking up to two hours, three times daily. We'd touch base regularly and some days Mark seemed positive - things seemed to be clicking. Other days he was flat-lined, still others: down. It was hard to know what was really happening as, per usual, the doctors said it could take weeks, if not months, to truly measure results. (My least favorite doctor lingo.) This two week period was good for me, though. I knew Mark was in a safe place with a strict routine and he had some drive to see it through. I took a stress break and hoped it would continue.

Mark did some journaling while he was gone. Actually he was pretty good about doing that periodically and it must have been nourishing to his soul. (I've since read everything I could find with

126

his writing on it, just again, to hear his heart.) His thoughts were encouraging to me from this time in Baja. He was in praise mode often, even if it was sacrificial praise. He processed some forgiveness issues and wrote of his thankfulness for his family and his redemption among other things.

And he came home with a box or two full of Baja concoctions to drink for the next month or so. It was always something.

*****

I would say there was a brief reprieve following the *Mexico experiment.* Mark's pain was not gone; his depression was not gone, but neither were either quite so extreme. We just walked tentatively forward always trying to be intentional about our steps. Mark would still be in bed more often than not, but he'd also rally occasionally to do something fun (like dinner with friends) or crazy (like climb on the roof to fix the swamp cooler).

All this sounds bizarre to me now as I frame into words our rollercoaster. How could Mark have been that bad? How could he do some of the things he did and truly be THAT BAD?

Only those who've walked in our shoes will understand the parallel realities happening at any given time, - ours since Mark's back surgery. They're really not explainable, but they're real, - the weaving in and out of what I can only now call wellness and oppression, sanity and insanity. Some days Mark was well in his mind, other days he was not; you never knew who/which would wake up in the morning. But again, Mark had a very strong mind and he fought for the sane and peaceful days. Some days he was just more successful than others.

*****

One day early Fall, when Mark was feeling more well and hopeful, he made plane reservations for he and I to go to Santa Barbara for Thanksgiving. Levi, Brandi and Bree would make it there by train and the plan was to finally grant my mom's wish for a big family Thanksgiving celebration in California. The Macs had talked about it for several years, but since the past three were post surgery (i.e. painful) and many previous Thanksgivings were either in Colorado or at our place in NM, we never quite made it happen. I so remember Mark at the computer wanting to press "confirm," for airfare, hesitant to do so. Should we step out in faith and breathe enough wellness into our circumstances (as though we could) to get there? Was this faith or presumption? Ahhh the head gymnastics of dealing with illness, - let alone mental illness. Mark wanted to make it happen. He wanted it for me. He said I deserved this long awaited family gathering. So "confirm" he did and we bought our tickets.

Per usual, there were fluctuations in how Mark felt that beautiful Indian Summer. Balancing meds seemed the biggest challenge, and between trying to keep the intake at a minimum (for health and cost reasons) and trying to ingest enough to get to the other side of Nardil, we just couldn't totally relax. All around us, people would wake up in the morning and do life - whatever that looked like for them. I'm not sure we were doing life... I don't know what we were doing.

*****

Sometime October-ish 2010, Mark took a good turn and, boy, were we excited. Physically he was still slow moving, still needed to ice his back, etc, - but mentally he was up. Twice friends invited us over for dinner to reunite with several others and we had such fun and *normal*. This was living. I think I can say Mark enjoyed the interaction and conversation and maybe, just maybe, was able to forget about his own circumstances for a brief time. Upon returning home after each dinner, though tired, we marveled at how well Mark felt and did. We hoped there were more outings ahead because that meant we *could*.

One day early (or was it mid?) November, Bree was home sick. Whenever my kids weren't feeling well I'd make them beds on the couch with everything they needed in reach on the coffee table. That way I could keep an eye on them and they could sleep or watch TV, or a movie, if they wanted. Mark was always really good with the kids when they were ill, better than I ever was. He had compassion down, I tell you, and was better than anyone I ever knew at caring for the sick and downtrodden. (I remember when Levi and Bree had their wisdom teeth pulled... Smile.) Anyway, Bree and I share a simple but vivid memory of Mark attending to her as she lay feverish on the couch. He brought her water and covered her with blankets. He sat briefly near her and pulled her damp hair away from her face. Besides one other, several hour stretch in December, this was the last peaceful, hopeful, normal site and night of Mark's life.

By the next morning everything had changed dramatically.

*****

I knew from the moment he walked out the bedroom door that something was terribly wrong. His eyes registered terror, his face and body anxiety. I couldn't imagine what had happened while I slept the night away, but Mark experienced a nightmare. A full blown demonic night terror. I asked him to tell me about it thinking the voicing of it would dispel the horror. I was pretty adept at downplaying the enemy's territory and hoped I could talk Mark out of the blackness that had overtaken him. But I couldn't.

I won't share the details of this dream. There are many things throughout the Mac story and my writing it out that I've chosen not to record. They're either so personal to the point of sacred or to speak of them would minimize their value. This is one of those times. As Mark was relating his dream, my skin began to crawl and I wanted to scream: Adversary, you DO NOT PLAY FAIR. - Which we all know. But sometimes it's just beyond belief what he's able to mess with in our lives. - Though I could calmly say, "It's just a stinkin' nasty dream, Mark," he couldn't shake it. And something cracked deep inside of him. A psychotic break? I don't know. But maybe.

Did we hit a point where the drug combination, or lack thereof, in Mark's body struck him down? Or was this spiritual? How much was a physical accumulation of pain, exhaustion and lots of inconsistent sleeping? If God has made anything clear to me over recent years it's this: no one will ever know the answers to these questions. And I need waste no time trying to figure them out; there will be no *figuring*.

*****

I kept waiting for a swing the other direction. Though the intensity of those few days following Mark's dream lessened some, he never got close to the day preceding it. Not close at all. And now Thanksgiving was approaching. We'd all been looking forward to our big California holiday and had entertained the notion, here and there, that it was going to be good. And we had tickets. And would it be any better not to go?

One more dangling hope that my sisters had been encouraging for a while was for Mark to get back out to Santa Barbara and check in to Cottage's mental health ward for a few days. 25 years ago that route brought new life; maybe it could again. There was a sad note (and a selfish concern) to that plan, however. Mark's 1986 treating doctor had recently been hit by a car while walking his dog and did not survive his injuries. I believe his death was a significant loss to the mental health community as well as to his family and certainly, to some degree, to the Macallisters. In any case, Mark was beyond desperate by this time; I was close on his heels so we decided to head to California and get Mark into the hospital – ASAP - upon landing in Santa Barbara.

Though it's difficult, I need to share here, that Mark began drinking after that nightmare. It's important to his story. I didn't recognize the drinking for what it was right away as I'd had no experience with it. I was pretty naive, but rightfully so. In all my years of knowing Mark, he never drank more than two or three beers over a football game. And that was rare. We shared a glass of wine over dinner occasionally. And that was rare. Mark never did drugs even during the height of the 60's and 70's drug culture. He was afraid of them. He saw what they did to his friends and he knew the damage (i.e. side effects, etc) from prescription drugs he had to take in his teen years. He tried marijuana once and it made him feel so weird that he never went there again. In all the years of taking Nardil and various other prescribed meds over time, Mark was always one to take less than prescribed. Never was he one to take more or to abuse drugs or alcohol. Drinking now was so indicative of his desperation. It was the only thing that took the edge off, he told me, once I figured out what was happening.

The closer we got to Thanksgiving, the worse Mark became. At some point, we made the decision that he needed to get to Santa Barbara like, yesterday, thus we changed his ticket to leave a couple days before the rest of us. My sisters were ready to collect him from the airport and get Mark to the hospital upon his arrival, but everything was happening so fast we didn't have much of a chance to think everything through. Mark was determined to hop on a plane, by himself, and get to California. Period.

But morning of departure wasn't so easy. And it was my wakeup to Mark's drinking. He was supposed to be checking in at the airport by 8:00 AM so when Bree and I discovered he was nowhere near ready to go at 7:00, I knew we were in trouble. And I knew Mark was drunk or in some similar state with a med/alcohol combination. So I began scrambling.

Bree made a big pot of coffee and we tried to get Mark to down it. - Does that even work? - We tried talking him in to postponing his flight or having one or both of us drive him the 30 minutes to the airport. He wouldn't have any of it. Guess that alcohol made him bold and, again, he was determined to do this deal for himself, by himself. I had seen Mark do all sorts of things under absolutely harrowing circumstances over the years and was pretty ready to let him do this one too - though very quickly, and certainly now, I'm wondering "what the heck was I thinking?"

He got in the car and left. For about two minutes, I was relieved. Then I panicked and quickly called a friend to pray. Before I even got off the phone I was getting an incoming call from Mark. "Come get me." He didn't make it off our hill before driving into a guardrail and disabling the car. Oh God, Oh God, Oh God.

*****

Bree and I weren't even dressed yet but we hopped in my vehicle with sweats and slippers and got Mark and his things from the side of the road about half a mile away. I drove. Mark sat silently in the passenger seat; Bree was making phone calls from the back to Mark's brother, Doug, - for his wisdom and decision-making advice; to Levi - to get him and his pastors to meet us at the airport. We needed help.

Levi was there when we arrived. Bree hopped out and my two amazing children escorted their out-of-control dad into the airport. - There's a story here all in itself, but... eventually, after skipping two outgoing flights, and accepting the kind help of a friend who

131

jumped on the plane and went with him, the two safely arrived in California and Mark was self-committed at Santa Barbara Cottage Hospital's Psychiatric Unit.

Meanwhile, back in New Mexico, I was barely keeping it together. I was relieved Mark was safe somewhere, but I was exhausted and spent in so many ways. I didn't know if I could keep going like this, to use Mark's words. But I had to. I was to fly out the following day; the kids were hopping on the train. Time was not standing still no matter how much I preferred that it did.

*****

Thanksgiving was pretty horrible. This wasn't the long, hoped for plan. Mark was hospitalized for three days - with no similarities to the health care of the 80's. The goal now was to get patients discharged as quickly as possible, criteria staged by insurance companies and over-crowded hospitals, I assume.

Mark was treated as an alcoholic. Try though we did to convince the doctors and nurses that the alcohol only presented in the past month, no one took any posture but one of dealing with a drunkard. All the "counseling" presented - and there was plenty of that - was towards detox and alcohol rehabilitation. It was maddening.

I understand how things looked upon Mark's admittance. I understand there wasn't enough time to provide what Mark likely needed since he didn't meet the criteria for staying: presenting endangerment to himself and/or others. - Actually he was in danger of harming himself, but he was also pumped full of hospital drugs that boosted him enough and he seemed better. So he was discharged prematurely and the days to follow got darker by the hour.

*****

The kids and I tried to enter in to the holiday festivities. My family was doing all they could to lighten our load and be supportive, but Mark was just an anxious wreck and it was taking a toll on everyone. He managed to find some alcohol and that didn't help, of course, because it wasn't what his system was really needing. He didn't get drunk again - ever - but the slightest bit made me a little crazy as I slid into my own despairing place. Mark took off on a couple walks when he wanted to jump out of his skin and it scared me to death. I imagined him walking in front of a bus or disappearing in the Santa Barbara hills never to be found. Ultimately he decided he couldn't participate in Thanksgiving dinner but promised to stay put, be a good boy, and allow the kids and me a few hours of peace and uninterrupted family time. But it was miserable for me - sorry family - and by that evening I knew something had to give.

I can't even adequately describe, in writing, what Mark's agony looked like, but I can only say I knew I had to get him back in the hospital. Santa Barbara wasn't going to take him. I had to get him back to Albuquerque.

*****

As much as Mark hated the hospital and everything it represented in his condition, he also recognized that he had to get there. It makes me cry to remember his desperation. He wanted to live; he wanted to get better and win this war. And somehow, somehow, Mark got on another plane, - by himself, and made his way back to Albuquerque where a friend picked him up and took him home. I had made all the arrangements, spending an entire day on the phone with UNM's hospital and various friends to care for Mark until I could follow him home a day later. It was a stinkin' nightmare as flights had to be changed and the hospital had to find Mark a bed. He couldn't go directly there. So I had three wonderful men lined up to stay with Mark for 24 hours. Nevertheless, when I met Mark at the hospital after landing in Albuquerque, he had made his first serious suicide attempt by downing hordes of prescription drugs he'd had at home - the meds he'd accumulated and never wanted to take for a long, long time.

*****

The floor nurse didn't actually believe Mark had taken all the pills he stated. She said he'd be dead if it were true. She didn't know Mark. Mark's body was an anomaly. What meds were supposed to calm him down, agitated him. Those that were meant to jilt him out of depression, laid him flat. But more than either scenario, most meds just didn't touch him - period.

Mark was in the hospital for about a week. The kids and I visited him and though it was very difficult seeing him there, glimmers of hope also presented. The hospital was medicating him with some drugs I'd never heard of and I thought I'd heard of everything. I always knew when Mark was a tiny bit better because he'd rise up and take charge some. Here was no different. He exerted his truths, the reality of his cyclothymic depression, and the 25 years of relative success on Nardil, - because, again, he was being treated for addiction. - Last time an alcoholic, this time drug dependent as he was admitted *under the influence* in a failed suicide attempt. Once some of his system was flushed out and he was stabilized by the doctors, his strong mind kicked in and he tried reasonable discussion with his caretakers. And thus the cycle again: it was time to discharge him from the hospital. No concern for endangerment to others or self-inflicted harm.

I knew differently.

*****

Were any of us alive in December? I can hardly remember anything beyond the darkness of our circumstances. I went to work. Bree went to school. Levi went on tour. We somehow got a Christmas tree up, but never got beyond putting the lights on. (Why is that a vivid memory?) Mark was home, alone, too much and it wasn't many days beyond his hospital departure that I returned from work to an empty house. And a note.

*****

As I'm writing, I'm processing through hindsight and thinking of many things I'd do differently. I have to take those thoughts captive - quickly - or I'll drive myself crazy. At the time, although I knew we were in a very precarious place, I also had hope. I had seen God pull Mark from the edge before. We had survived great storms of trouble, and terror, and darkness. In the back of my mind, I felt just as strongly that this season would lift as I considered Mark might take his own life. - This was my mindset all along, until I didn't have the option.

So Mark was alone, at home, planning to leave us. I may have kept that note somewhere; I'm not sure. Essentially though, it said the same mantra, "I can't do this anymore." I called a couple friends immediately and punched Mark's number into my phone every couple minutes. Nothing. The police were called and came. It felt like something in the movies: a couple squad cars out front; officers walking the neighborhood looking for clues; friends fanning in and out of the house; multiple phone conversations taking place on multiple phones simultaneously. The police encouraged us that Mark was probably okay. Leaving notes is actually a good thing, and Mark took his computer with him and his phone. If he was serious about ending his life, this wasn't the norm.

At some point, Mark called. He wouldn't say where he was and, of course, the police tried to track his location so we tried to keep him talking. Bree and I. Bree was the champion. She spoke words of love and hope, sometimes with a firm, "Dad. You need to come home now. Mom needs you. Levi and I need you." The police were coaching her, floating notes in front of her face with instruction. I was often on my phone with Levi who was on tour, states away, agonizing over his absence while his family was in this monstrous scenario. A couple times Mark hung up, or said he had to go, and Levi would quickly interject with his own phone call. Thankfully he kept his dad on the phone for several stretches so we could take a breather on our end. - Ultimately, after several hours, Mark was finally convinced to halt whatever life-ending measures he was taking. He was obviously in some kind of stupor - drug and alcohol induced? - and confessed he'd slit his wrist, but he'd botched it and had it wrapped up. He didn't want to die.

Though his mind was coming back into focus, he still wouldn't tell us where he was and we had to settle for that for the night. The police told us all this business of tracking phone calls was way more successful in the movies than ever in real life and they could not pinpoint Mark's whereabouts. You'd think that would have been a horrific night but Bree and I were exhausted and fell asleep as dead men, ourselves. Not sure Levi fared so well, but we all got some rest and woke to another day.

The police didn't return but they checked in with us a couple times over the following hours. The kids and I talked sporadically with Mark on the phone, but until he was ready to reveal his whereabouts, we were at his mercy for connecting. Though I really had no idea where we'd land, I somehow relaxed a bit knowing Mark was communicating and wasn't shutting us out entirely.

Come evening I had a good friend of mine up to sit with me and keep me company. As the night grew later, she and I both talked to Mark on the phone and finally convinced him to tell us where he was. Immediately after, the police were called and dispatched to some hotel about 20 miles east of us. We got a phone call that an ambulance met them there, that Mark was not in very good shape but that he'd survive and be committed back into the hospital. I notified the kids and Bree hopped in a car and took off to meet Mark. I couldn't. I didn't have an ounce of energy or ability left in me. My friend stayed with me awhile longer and I remember her saying something to the effect, "If he takes off again, he won't survive it." She wasn't being negative; she just caught a glimpse of our reality.

*****

Mark took a turn or two for the better being in the hospital again. All those wonderful, not-to-leave-the-building drugs were kicking in. Still he was nowhere near well, this time, and condemning voices were stacking accusations against him like crazy. "Look at all you're putting your family through." "You're bleeding your life savings dry." "You've become an embarrassment." "Really? You? A pastor?" And then the, "You'll never be well. This is your lot in life, don't you know?"

Bree made the initial hospital appearance so Mark would know family was near; then Levi was home again, and he and I did the follow up seeing Mark during visiting hours. Nothing we said brought any light to Mark's eyes. Nothing made him smile. It was so incredibly hard. And one more time, discharge approached and I knew we were no better off than before. Levi and I actually met with hospital supervisors and begged them to keep Mark longer. I think we may have gained a couple days, but no more.

Christmas was maybe a week away and I changed my game plan a little. I was still working so I lined up friends to be with Mark each day for the few hours I couldn't. He hated that, too, but I couldn't leave him alone. A couple times folks came to our house; a couple times I'd drop Mark off in town at a friend's. I was thankful I had a few days off for the holidays as this navigating was stressful for me. It's crazy that I continued working at all, but my workplace didn't know what was going on at this point, and my job actually provided me with some much needed relief from my daily circumstances. It wasn't the best case scenario, but it tied us over.

And then Christmas Eve arrived and we, four Macallisters, celebrated the birthday of our Savior in a sweet and miraculous way. Levi was asked to do some Scripture reading at church that late afternoon and we went. Mark rose to the occasion. We drove to town and were not disappointed as the service was beautiful - all worship and Scripture readings. One of those reverent, awe-inspiring occasions when you're reminded of God's majesty and gentleness interwoven in a babe's flesh. Though we didn't stick around after to mingle, we still enjoyed each other's company back at home for a couple more hours sitting around the dinner table doing our traditional Christmas Eve meal. Mark prayed and smiled and laughed and I'll treasure that memory forever as it was the last happy one the four of us had.

*****

Christmas Day was not happy. We tried to pull it off, but whatever wonderful reprieve was granted us yesterday was absent today. I know Mark was doing his best not to be the downer, but his energy to not be was gone. He sat in his chair and unwrapped a present or two with a glazed look in his eyes, unable to maintain any family conversation we were attempting. So as soon as the obligatory gift unwrapping concluded, the kids were off to happier places and Mark back to bed.

*****

For the next several days I was either working and toting Mark to town to essentially be supervised, or I was off work and keeping an eye on him myself. But I was beyond depleted across the board. And Mark was back to erratic state - sometimes sleeping all day and awake pacing the floors all night. I resorted to taking sleeping pills, myself, as I couldn't skip sleep and make it through my days. I hated doing that because I really had no idea what Mark might do in the night hours, but I trusted - somehow - that The Lord wouldn't allow things to get too crazy while I slept. (*Too* is relative, I learned.)

There's not much about this time that I remember clearly,

except that it was gray. Just dull and dim and difficult. New Year's Day rolled around, and though I've never been a big fan of the holiday, this one was the worst. The kids were gone (Levi wasn't living at home anyway and Bree was with friends) and Mark was disturbingly agitated. He said he needed to get out of the house for a little while and was going for a walk. If I'd had the energy to back him down I would have, but I didn't, so out he went only to call me a short while later saying he was driving out of town. - Long story, short. I eventually got him to come home all the while wanting to crawl in a hole somewhere myself.

*****

New Year's Day fell on Saturday and on January 3rd I was back at work. Mark was relegated to friends/sitters who kept an eye on him for me, but it was down-right horrible to drop him off and leave him. By now I couldn't really relax at work anymore; where would this end? We couldn't continue like this day after day.

After Mark's second hospitalization - since he didn't meet inpatient criteria - a suicide prevention counselor was recommended. We went, but there was nothing at all hopeful about our meeting. The prospective was, "Sometime down the road a ways, you'll feel better," essentially. Why were we not being heard? Why didn't anyone hear us say, "We're one foot off the ledge NOW?" My bigger fear to be honest, was not suicide however, but that Mark and I would exist in this horrific reality forever. Unless you've lived it, you have no idea. I confessed this bigger agony to my close friends who literally held me up daily with their love and support and prayers. I didn't want Mark to die; I didn't want him to live like this either. Unless God had a miraculous rescue in mind, I saw no way out. Long term plans for recovery were inconceivable and I knew it.

January 5th I was a little late getting out of work. The imaging techs had a problem with a patient and since I was the late worker, I had to wait and close up after everyone left. I texted Mark to say I'd pick him up as soon as possible. I think my delay only amounted to 30 minutes or so, but I could tell when I arrived to get him that he was using every ounce of his strength to be still. We hopped in the car and headed home quickly. When we arrived, he went straight into the spare bedroom and I didn't hear him

138

for awhile. Bree came home and she and I sat on the couch most of the evening. I don't remember if we ate or did anything else, but I know Mark got on the phone and called his psychiatrist and asked if it'd be okay if he doubled up on his meds that night. The doctor said no.

I didn't go in to say goodnight to Mark. When I didn't hear him again after his phone conversation with the doctor, I had hoped he'd fallen asleep. I didn't want to chance waking him up if that were the case. If it wasn't, I couldn't face him. If I have regrets, this is one of them: that I didn't go to him that night, that he was alone.

Bree and I went to bed, she to a nightmare about Mark leaving in the night, me to another dead sleep. And when I awoke in the morning, Mark was gone.

*****

I didn't know it at first. I started my daily routine, but at some point I peeked into Mark's room to find the bed made up and no note anywhere. I immediately looked into the driveway to discover the car was gone (our only vehicle since Mark's accident prior to Thanksgiving). I woke Bree up and it wasn't but minutes later that the phone rang and it was Mark. "Jody. The car is in the Four Hills parking lot. I can't stay, Jody. I love you and the kids. I can't die at home with dignity. I have to go away; I'm getting on a bus and headed out of town. Don't try to find me, I'm leaving now." And that was it.

You might wonder why he had access to the car. I don't know myself. Right after Mark's first hospitalization in Albuquerque, the kids and I took away his car keys and wallet. We removed a couple guns and knives from the house that we'd had from our Ranch days. I hid his passport and anything else I could possibly think of that would allow an exit of any kind. What happened? I've racked my brain and the only thing I come up with is: without thinking, I automatically hung my car keys on the hook just inside the door when we walked in the previous night. My own mind was so distracted that I could have done that. Mark's mind was so focused on a way out that he would have quietly noticed.

*****

I didn't call the police this time. I called a few friends who were already interceding faithfully for the Macallisters and who would step it up for us as needed. I had to inform Mark's caretaker for the day and he immediately hopped in his car and visited the bus station asking questions of ticket agents, etc. One of my friends came to the rescue and drove me to town, to Four Hills where we found the car right where Mark said it would be. I had Mark's keys I'd hidden long ago; when I unlocked the door, there were mine. And Mark's phone.

So he had no wallet, no ID, no credit cards, no phone and no keys.

Can you believe I made it through work that day? I still wasn't ready to reveal my scenario there, thus I had no choice but to plow forward. Plus, if this continued to be my lot I had to keep going somehow. I was well trained, by this time, to put one foot in front of the other.

When I got home that evening, to a dark and empty house, I didn't know quite what to do. I couldn't invite the police squad out again. And what could they do anyway? Less than the last time since Mark didn't have a phone on him. I needed to call family, which I did, but they couldn't do anything either. And it was so exhausting retelling the story and answering questions and - thinking.

It was an interesting night, I remember. I was sort of hungry, but couldn't work a meal in what with all the phone calls. I booted up my laptop in the kitchen and was thinking maybe, maybe if Mark got to an internet cafe somewhere, he'd message me. The computer loaded and I was mildly startled to see Mark's login and name pop up as though most recent user. I was the last one on; Mark never used my computer. Before I had a chance to get any further, the phone rang again and I decided to stretch out on my bed for a bit. Just as I was finishing the call I heard the computer's shut-down tune. I walked into the kitchen just as it was powering off. Was the battery low? No. It was plugged in.

It felt a little eerie. But more than that, I interpreted what happened as a "You're exhausted; go to bed, Jody," from Mark. There was nothing else I could do. I waited for Bree to get home, we talked briefly and then I crawled into bed.

That night I had a vivid dream about Mark. I dreamt that he was gone again, but he called me and told me where he was. He told me he wasn't coming home; I could come see him, though, if I wanted. He gave me directions to a house so I hopped in the car and drove straight there. I don't know where this house was exactly. Stylistically it could have been an Albuquerque home, but I don't think that's important. What was important is that when I pulled alongside this house, Mark was working in the yard, shovel in hand, dressed in his old, blue-green work shorts. When he saw me at the curb, he looked up and smiled the smile I loved. He was well. I knew it. He was healthy and whole and well. I got out of the car and Mark walked towards me, smiling all the way. He told me he was happy and working to landscape the yard at this house. He wasn't coming home again. He had work to do.

And that was it. He didn't touch me, nor I him. There were no goodbyes. Just glowing wellness and smiles. I actually don't think I said a word, - I just watched him approach me in health and I listened to his words. I wasn't sad in my dream. I was just happy he was well. I was happy he was happy.

*****

Waking up from that dream wasn't so happy. Getting out of bed the next morning wasn't so easy either except for the fact that I couldn't sleep another minute. My mind was racing, my mind was dull. My heart was anxious, my heart was numb. How does that work? Thus began 18 surreal days.

I knew I couldn't be making and returning phone calls all day and night long, so I implemented group messaging on my phone and tried to bring all the faithful prayer supporters into my loop immediately. The feedback, love and support I received sustained me - again. People began bringing meals to the house. I got cards and letters in the mail and encouragement via email. Some of my closest friends and several folks overseas still made phone calls so I could hear their voices, I suppose. I needed that, too.

I went to work every day. And every day I sent a morning

and evening group text to maybe 100 people telling them I had not heard from Mark and had nothing new to report. I shared on the nights when temperatures dipped below freezing that I worried about Mark being cold. Mostly I just thanked people for standing with me in the unknown.

At some point, I did call the police, maybe four or five days into Mark's absence. I talked to the kids about it first, because I had talked to them about not calling police initially. We agreed we needed to not stress and strain forward, for our own wellness, but after a few days we decided if Mark were to be found dead, we had better notify someone before that happened. Somebody needed to know someone cared. - A detective was put on the case. Groan.

The other thing I did was speak to my manager at work finally. She was totally supportive and said I could take family leave immediately, that there were provisions for this kind of *hardship*. I was grateful for the option, but chose to plod on. I didn't think sitting at home would help anything.

*****

Day in, day out. No word. The detective was young and learning the ropes. I honestly don't know if he knew any more than I did about how to find a missing person. We'd talk every day or two and I had questions he had to check on before replying. I'm not criticizing or complaining, I'm just saying we were a team, of sorts, trying to brainstorm possibilities for a grown man's disappearance.

My parents came out for a week to stay with Bree and me. They were worried about us - understandably so. We talked about Mark and wondered how long the silence would last. We pondered the idea of him roaming right under our noses, but in choosing to be hidden, he was. We also verbalized the possibility that he was no longer among us at all.

A night or two before my parents left to head back to California, a bunch of friends gathered at our home in Cedar Crest to pray, - pray for Mark, pray for me, pray for answers and relief and God's presence to be known. It was a tough night for me as these events had a tendency to burst the surreal and penetrate reality. This was defining. But I felt better, a lot better, by the time everyone left.

142

God had shown up and He was definitely in control. And He was/is Loving and Good.

*****

I put my parents on the westbound train and another detective came on our case the same day. She and I talked the hard stuff; she knew the answers to my questions. Like: Have morgues been called and what happens when nameless missing persons show up somewhere? I don't know where this gal had been, but I felt like we were moving again.

She wanted us to have a DNA sample on file in case they found Mark, dead or alive, for identity purposes. And she needed two sources. This idea was tossed around for a couple days as Mark's mom had to be included and we weren't sure how she would do with this. Her health (both mental and physical) wasn't great and I honestly doubted her ability to cooperate. Thankfully, although I don't know that she fully understood the process, we set up a residence visit with the Glendora, CA police to get a mouth swab from her. Levi was to be our second source.

I feel the weight of those days as I remember them now, over three years later, - what we were asking a mother and a son to do.

*****

Jan 24, 2011. I got the facility information for Levi and told him where to go. The detective would call Glendora and dispatch their folks there. We would have all the DNA required by the end of the day. But we didn't end up needing it.

I was driving to work when I got the phone call. "Mrs Macallister? Are you home? Detective Benton and I would like to meet you there shortly. We're fairly certain we've found your husband."

*****

I quickly called Levi to abort his errand and get him headed to the mountains. Bree was with a friend, so I called her, too. After phoning work, I also turned around and joined my children for a meeting I didn't sign up for. Never did I sign up for this. No one in their right mind would.

It took a while for the two detectives to arrive. Levi, Bree and I talked a little. There wasn't much to say; I was worried for my kids, what their hearts and minds were experiencing in the moment. They were worried for me and mine.

And then, suddenly, it was over. We knew the story. Mark had been Home since - estimated time-of-death - January 7th, 2011. He never left Albuquerque; he went to a motel room and took his life. Just like that. And because he had no ID on him, he waited in a morgue for over two weeks until someone made the right phone call, i.e. until God's sovereign timing said, "Enough" and rescued the Mac wife and children from unbearable uncertainty.

That day was close to three and a half years ago now. And yesterday was Easter, Mark. And I missed you. I missed your presence and your voice mingling with others in worship: I missed your laughter amongst family gathered to celebrate the Resurrection and to enjoy one another.

And I couldn't help but feel, still, as one displaced and out of sync with my reality. Maybe I won't ever be, shouldn't ever be synced, in this life. I'm not HOME yet; this world isn't my home; I'm just journeying through.

At the same time, I am well, Mark. God's grace has proven sufficient over and over again. He has faithfully been at my side when I've done so many things I never thought I could do without you. Like selling our home. And moving. And attending to cars. And sitting with a financial consultant. And, and, and... I suppose a lot of women do all those things on their own, but I never thought I would; never wanted to. Yet our lives together prepared me. You challenged me, directly and indirectly, Mark, to keep my eyes on Jesus, to trust Him for my every need, to long for Him like the watchman for the morning.

You'd be so proud of your children, Mark. Levi and Bree are amazing. Their hearts have triumphed over our story with hope and generosity and by that I mean: they give themselves to others. They share their journey and offer the hope that's been given them. They've blossomed since you left us, - by the grace of God they are shining lights.

Despite all the really hard years we experienced together, Mark, I'm glad God gave me the honor of being your wife. I'm glad for all the wonderful, beautiful times when you were well and we enjoyed life and growing together. I'm glad for the extravagant wealth of opportunity we shared in working side by side - for His Kingdom - most of our married days. I'm glad for the Mac Four and our precious little family.

And I'm glad too, Mark, for my heavenly assignment - to love you "for better or for worse, for richer, for poorer, in sickness and in health," as faithfully as I was able while you dwelt on earth. I wasn't always good at it, but God enabled me to finish when I, so often, felt unable.

You taught me so much, Mark, and God taught me so much through you. I will forever be thankful. Thank you, Father, Lover of my soul. Thank you, Mark, His gift to me on this journey of joy.

EPILOGUE

Nine months after Mark's move to Heaven, I took Bree to Asia. It was a trip Mark meant to make with her and I knew it was important that she didn't miss out. For three weeks we traipsed around Thailand, Malaysia, Myanmar, China and Hong Kong, visiting places, visiting people Mark loved. Places and people into which he poured his life. We had so much fun; it was a trip of a lifetime and a precious memory now that I'll treasure forever.

I was a little worried before going that Bree might get restless meeting with people she'd never seen before. I figured she'd enjoy the travel, the sites, the adventure of it all; I also knew we needed to connect with people whom Mark loved and who loved him. My immeasurable blessing, after it was all said and done, was Bree saying her favorite part of the trip was hearing the stories about her dad from some who had known him longer than she had. It was good for her to learn about Mark's heart and passion up close, - something it's just hard to fathom this side of the ocean. She needed to walk the roads, breathe the air, touch the people. And God did it. He showed up and did something wonderful and healing in us both.

Before we went to Asia, Bree and I moved to California to be near my family in Santa Barbara. Bree went to school and dug in for about 18 months before heading back to New Mexico. She missed her friends, her community and her brother. I don't blame her a bit; I get it. Levi and Brandi declared Albuquerque home base (after marrying in April 2011) and though they're on the road much of the year, they've recently bought a house and are attempting more strategic traveling so as to be home more often.

I'm still in Santa Barbara for the time being: working, enjoying parents, sisters and their families and a church I've grown to love. And Santa Barbara is a paradise on earth. I know God's had me here for a reason and for a season. I'm not sure what's next.

But one thing I DO know: God has a plan for me. He's not finished. Sometimes I've stumbled into believing He might be. Not that it's His heart, just my tripped-up mind saying, "I've had my turn; it's now someone else's," as though God had limited plans and resources and sometimes they run out this side of Heaven. Oh my. Nothing could be further from the truth.

Tomorrow I would have celebrated 30 years of marriage with Mark. As a young bride I envisioned a very different scenario than the one I'm now living. It's hard to reconcile sometimes. I tell everyone, "This is not the story I would have written." In all honesty, I don't like this one much. I would have preferred a "happily ever after" to complete my fairy tale beginning. Wouldn't we all?

But God's ways are not our ways.

God's ways are higher – "as the heavens are higher than the earth, so are His ways higher than ours. " (Isaiah 55:9) I don't understand them. I can't. Yet, "I know Whom I have believed in and am persuaded that He is able to keep that which I've committed unto Him until that Day." (2 Tim 1:12) And that is enough.

To Him be all Glory, and Honor, and Power forever. Amen.

*****

When I first felt God prompting me to write this story, I was certain Levi and Bree were to be a part of it. This is their story, too. And their children's. And as I said early on: God has used their generous sharing of it to help others and to extend the love and hope of Jesus to those hurting like they've hurt. This is what God does (2 Corinthians 1:3-5)!

To Write Love on Her Arms (www.twloha.com), a non-profit organization that offers hope and help for people struggling with addictions, mental illnesses and suicide, graciously produced a video, years back, giving Levi and Bree a platform to first share their story. This book is simply another opportunity, and what follows is their contribution…

150

BREE'S STORY

In the last days, when things were at their worst and desperation took hold of my dad's spirit, he claimed he would do whatever it took to alleviate the burden he believed he'd become on our family. He'd move to Asia, he'd disappear, he'd live on the streets. And in those few weeks he was missing, I'd imagine him curled up and sleeping under a bridge somewhere. It's a thought that flashes in my mind even now from time to time, and it's haunting.

Not long ago, I ran across a man with shaggy, white hair and shadowed, blue eyes. A prominent, curved nose. High cheek bones and sagging skin. He asked me for money for a cup of coffee, and I took him inside a shop to buy him one. He might have been someone's daddy, and at the very least he was someone's son.

"Thanks, Sweetie." And his mouth turned up into a tired smile. I saw the hints of crow's feet at the corners of his eyes and a sparkle that begged to shine through. My mind immediately took in the man's every feature and altered it just slightly to become the man I knew growing up. He was tall. 6'2." His hair was short when it was kept up, peppered black and white, growing whiter all the time. His big toothed smile stretched all the way to his bright blue eyes, the years etching lines in their corners. He had a prominent, curved nose and high cheek bones. Most of my life he had a beard, once clean shaven that I can remember, and a season with a handlebar mustache. I preferred the full beard.

151

He asked my permission when he shaved it. He told a story about how his brother once shaved his own without telling his family beforehand; his daughter cried for a whole day, having not recognized him at first. My dad learned through observation as well as experience. He didn't have to learn everything the hard way. Most things, maybe, but not everything. He was considerate and thought of others in everything he did. Maybe even too much, now that I think about his reason for going away.

He said that he thought it would be easier on us if he wasn't around. In his mind, he thought he was loving us. That, sure, we'd miss him for six months then we'd get over it. He was that specific. Six months. Well, Dad, we're almost four years in and we're not over it. And even though we aren't over it, we are okay. I think you'd be proud of all of us. And I think you'd see how much we love you, - how much we always have.

*****

When I was six, my parents bought me a pink tricycle. We lived at The Ranch just outside of Lancaster, California, and it was my birthday. April 1st. Dad sent me to my room to get something, and when I came back out to the kitchen, there it was. This shiny, new trike. I was so excited. I rode it around the kitchen thinking it was the best present I could have ever gotten. I remember the joy in my dad's face at bringing me happiness.

It's beautiful to recognize how that impression held true to his character. My dad was a man who truly found joy in the joy of others.

He loved to periodically surprise our family with special treats or small trips. Sometimes he'd show up at school and bring me a York candy or money for lunch. On one occasion, dad surprised our family with a trip to Big Bear to play in the snow. We stayed in a friend's cabin and I stuck my finger in a light socket on accident. I remember watching cartoons in the morning and going on drives or walks in the afternoon. There was a wraparound porch on the house and I fed a squirrel that frequented the property. Dad's surprises were always fun, always special, always intentional.

It was at Big Bear that I first lied to my parents. It was dinner time and I was hungry. When asked if I washed my hands before

152

sitting down, I blurted out "Yes!" a little too quickly and Dad was suspicious. He asked me again, and I said yes again. Dad probably never actually believed me, but he chose to trust me, anyway, and let the rest play out. The guilt settled in around bedtime and weeks went by before I finally confessed. It was then that Dad and Mom sat on my bed with me while I cried. Dad talked to me about forgiveness and second chances, yet emphasized the importance of telling the truth. He hugged me all the while and told me that my lingering guilt had been punishment enough. He told me, as he did with high frequency throughout my life, that being alone - anywhere - is the worst place to be. He hated that I had been alone in my own head and that it had tortured me.

In my early years, I invited Mom and Dad into most everything I was going through. Dad tucked me in to bed every night, and most nights asked if there was anything I wanted to talk about. It seemed like the most normal thing in the world to me, but I realize he did it because it was the farthest thing from normal during his childhood. He was always alone in his thoughts, and he wanted to make sure I wasn't.

*****

My family was lucky enough to be on the road often. Whether for a missions outreach, retreat, or just a family vacation, I was able to see a lot and do a lot from an early age. Our family made several trips to San Francisco over the years where we stayed on Haight and Ashbury in the "Haight House." House members would make food to be distributed to the homeless living on the streets. We would go out with a rolling cart and serve these people and give them gospel tracts. I loved being on the streets in the thick of the action, reading the tracts to myself and talking to the people coming for food. I was fascinated by their appearance and mannerisms. I witnessed my first arrest on the streets of San Francisco when I was no older than seven. A man was cuffed by two undercover cops and his girlfriend was a shrieking mess, falling to the ground and sobbing, pleading with the officers to let her boyfriend go. My dad explained that the man had broken probation by being in that part of the city. After we passed out food, we welcomed those who were interested to come back to the house and take a shower and clean up. We had mini worship meetings at night and there were always new faces. I never thought anything strange of these trips and the things I experienced

153

growing up. In hindsight, it was probably not the most common thing for two little kids to be as involved as we were in often dangerous environments. But that's what life looked like with two parents dedicated to full time ministry. And I couldn't be more thankful.

Before things got bad, my dad really was everything I needed him to be, when I needed him to be it. When I'd get mad, he'd hold a pillow in front of his stomach and tell me to go to town. When I was happy he'd pull me into a big hug and celebrate with me. When I was sad, he'd put me on his lap and hold me.

In middle school came my first puppy-love heartbreak. Details aside and ultimately irrelevant, I will never forget my dad's response to the situation. He sat and cried with me and validated my 11 year old feelings that even I felt ridiculous in acknowledging. He told me that I was allowed to be sad and hurt, regardless of how old I was. He told me that he hoped and prayed that one day I would give another boy a shot, and that I wouldn't let this situation harden me. "It won't always happen like this, Honey." He didn't call me silly. He didn't say I was too young. He sat and listened and agreed that it sucked. That meant a lot to me at the time. And now.

And on the subject of love, my dad was cheesy; and while having a daughter terrified him, he tried so hard. So hard. He created memories for me and took me on "daddy-daughter dates" as often as he could. It was on one of these dates that we chose the song we'd dance to on my wedding day. It remains the only thing I have planned for my someday-wedding. It's a song we loved, and actually did get the chance to dance to together once. He took me to a purity ball when I was 12 and taught me how to dance.

It's helpful for me to write everything out in this way. It helps me remember the good. There was a lot of good. And however fragmented, these pieced together stories represent who he was.

I know that my dad lived with a lot of guilt. I never knew it at the time, but I know it now. So a lot of the things he taught me and modeled for me in different ways make more sense now. One of the things I value the most from my memories of him was his emphasis that something could be "all done." Whether personally broken about my own shortcomings or mistakes, or whether I'd done something to warrant some sort of reprimand or correction, my dad always made sure I could let it go when it was all done.

I got in trouble as I was growing up just like any other kid. Dad (and Mom) always explained why I was in trouble and why I was being punished and how I was actually being loved through it. Every time. After I got in trouble, he would hold me and tell me that he loved me. He would stay through my tears and then tell me, "It's all done." He would tell me until I believed it. He knew that correction was sometimes necessary, but he also knew that he wanted his little girl to be able to let it go. Whatever it was. He would ask me how I felt and usually my response was "shaky." He would ask me periodically until I wasn't shaky anymore. He'd say, "It's all done." And I would finally say, "It's all done." And then he'd never bring it up again.

Up to this point, I haven't even begun to describe how and when and why things went south. Interesting, because at the start of this endeavor, all I could remember was the bad.

The last time I saw Dad completely well was sometime during the fall of 2010. I was sick and he took care of me, the way daddies do. I was lying on the couch in our Cedar Crest home, as was the natural resting place for a sick Macallister kid. For most of the day Dad sat at the foot of the couch with my feet rested on his lap. We watched TV and ate macaroni and cheese (definitely the best sick food). He got me juice and water refills, put in new movies once one was finished, and held the pan for me when my stomach did its thing. He brushed my hair out of my face with his big, callused hands and told me how much he hated it when I didn't feel good.

He served me happily all day and his eyes were clear. It was the last time I ever saw him that way.

That night he had a nightmare that I won't get into, but his panicked voice is what woke me early the next morning. It was like he'd been taken over. After that night he was never the same.

Sometimes the hurt in my heart is unbearable when I think about how many times my dad's chest must have ached from the neglect he received from me. After he died, my brother got into his Facebook account and I read one of the outgoing messages he'd sent to my mom while he was in Mexico for another treatment trial. It said "How is Bree doing? She didn't answer my call... Tell her I love her." I turned my back on him so many times. Where he sat with me in my pain, hugged me, kissed me, loved me, I left the house. I could never understand. And I punished him for his already existing pain. If I could have one more chance, I'd answer on the first ring.

I don't remember what I was doing the first time my dad disappeared. I was in Albuquerque and when my mom called me to ask if I'd heard from him, I knew something was wrong. There had been threats before. Passive threats like, "I can't live like this" and, "I can't do this anymore." My mom told me that he left a letter and that it was serious. I hung up the phone and drove to where my best friend was. She was having dinner with a another friend from out of town, but came and met me in the parking lot to hear my random mumblings of what I thought was going on. In hindsight, I had to have looked crazy to her. My dad had disappeared and had written quite clearly that he would not be back, and I stood in the middle of a parking lot blank-faced with a blatant inability to discern what I should do. Brittany hugged me and told me to go home.

Oh. Duh.

So I went home. There were police officers wandering around in the dark with light from their flashlights bobbing along the ground. I walked past them in a daze and into my living room where more police officers gathered around the dining room table with Mom. And by the way, my mom will always be my earthly vision of strength. I could see the worry and helplessness on her face, but I could also see the determination.

I read the letter and my mom called my brother who was touring at the time. I felt terrible for Mom for having to break that kind of news, terrible for my brother for being too far away to be with us, and terrible for me. Because it was terrible.

There were too many police officers. They bothered me. One kept saying that he needed to check the garage again and that thought just horrified me. I asked him if that really made any sense. That someone would leave a letter for his family to seemingly spare them finding him only to make it as far as the garage. The policeman said that I'd be surprised. I wanted to punch him.

Another, more sensitive officer said that Dad was likely still alive. That in his experience, people determined to end their own life didn't leave notes, didn't take with them their computers and cell phones.

It was then that my dad called. I don't remember if it was Mom or I that answered and spoke to him first, just that I spent a great deal of time on the phone with him. I don't remember everything that I said, probably because half was fed to me through one of the officers via his little notepad. All that mattered was that Dad stay on the phone. He just kept saying how sorry he was, but that there wasn't another way, that he was convinced of that now. He hung up and called back multiple times throughout the evening but refused to tell us where he was. His cell phone couldn't be traced. Hours later, the police had cleared out and it was me and my mom. What a long night. When the phone calls stopped, in the late night darkness, we were left to our imaginations.

The next day he called again, and we breathed again. He still refused to tell us where he was and he sounded weak. I don't remember anything that happened that day. Only what came that night. I was out but on my way back home when he called my mom again and told her that he'd hurt himself. He finally told her where he was, - somewhere in Edgewood at a hotel that didn't ask for his personal information. I got home and by that time my mom had already called the police with his whereabouts. We didn't know how bad Dad was, but had hope that he would be found in time. And hope that he didn't want to die after all.

When word came that he had been picked up and was being transported to the hospital, I told my mom that I was ready to go. She decided not to join me, a fact that may appear selfish or uncaring to onlookers, but I get it. The relief she had to have felt, I believe, matched her tiredness. And she deserved a rest. She had a friend over and that friend loved on her while I went to the hospital to see my daddy.

He and I had a rocky relationship. We clashed quite a bit and I was as irrationally angry with him as he was with the rest of the world when his mind wasn't clear. It still never occurred to me to not go to the hospital. I called my best friend, Aaron, and he agreed to go with me. He drove to the emergency wing of UNM, a place I'd grown much too familiar with years before. I spoke with the woman at the front desk and she confirmed that Mark Macallister had been checked in but, given his condition, was apparently unable to let me through those ominous double doors to see him. Looking back, I don't understand how a daughter with valid identification could be refused the right to see her father, but it was something I apparently didn't push enough to make happen. In the end, I just somehow wanted him to know that I'd been there. That he wasn't alone. Growing up, he never wanted that for me and I guess that's the part that influenced me to stay. I prayed and sat with Aaron and waited. A few minutes passed and I saw blurs of activity on the other side of the doors where patients were admitted. I stood up and walked to them just close enough to push through if the internally controlled locks weren't activated. I saw him there, then, on a hospital bed surrounded by nurses. He was awake but looked weak. He looked old. I willed him to look at me but didn't see his eyes move in my direction. I stood there until he was wheeled away. At that point I assumed my chance was gone and it was safe to go back home. Aaron was my safety net then. He affirmed that I'd done all I could do at that point and prayed for me as we walked back to the car. It was only a few minutes later that I received a text from my dad's number that said, "Bree? Was that you? Were you here?" My heart broke and lifted all at once and I said, "Yes, Daddy. You are not alone. I came to see you. I'll be there as soon as they'll let me in." I went to sleep that night knowing that at least for now, he was safe.

It was the next day that my dad was admitted to the psychiatric unit of UNM. I only distinctly remember going to visit him once; visiting hours were limited and he wasn't there long. Still, the thought makes me sad that I didn't go every day. Again, I had a friend drive me to see him. Something about emotional driving concerned my mom enough to where she always wanted someone with me those days. Ironically, my emotions had been absent from the situation for years already. I was essentially unfeeling except for the constant hum of anxiety just under my numbed surface.

I was allowed in the common area to meet him. He was in sweats. I remember his eyes, bright blue, pleading to sparkle like they did when he was whole. There was a hint of him beneath his burdens. My conversation with him that day begged to break through the barrier and cause him to talk to me. There were moments. There were. And it was those moments that I try to hold onto. Dad seemed to soak in every word of love and forgiveness and hope that I had to give to him. It was only after I had repeated myself a dozen times that I got up to leave. I wrapped my arms around his big belly that was growing smaller all the time and turned to walk away. After the double doors had closed I looked back and saw the tears rolling down his face.

Christmas 2010 was awful. It just was. I camped out in Levi's room as per our tradition. We tried to make it as normal as possible. As a kid I remember Levi and I waking up early on Christmas morning and waiting as long as we could stand it before going to wake our parents. We wanted the day to last as long as possible. Obviously, as you get older, Christmas loses some of its much-anticipated magic, but this year it was especially obvious that things just weren't like they used to be. Mid-morning we went to the kitchen and made coffee. Mom came out shortly after and we set up a spot on the floor for my dad, although I remember him opting for his recliner for a while at least. We had breakfast and sat in the living room opening presents. There were a few for each of us, but I don't remember much except the feeling of heaviness in the room. I had gotten my dad a notebook with the "Footsteps in the Sand" poem embossed on the front. I thought that maybe, if he journaled some, it would at least help the emotional side of his ailments. That with the poem's reminder that Jesus carries us when we're weak... It was a ridiculous present but it was literally the only thing I could think of at that point.

Every year since Levi was born, my dad would receive a coffee mug with our pictures on it from us. It was his favorite present every year, although he always acted like it was a total surprise. We got him another mug that year and I remember him smiling a little. It was a smile for us though. He was trying, but he was empty.

*****

January 5, 2011. Five, the number of Grace. The last day I saw my dad. I stayed home that day and sat in the living room as he wandered restlessly around the house until my mom took him to town where someone could keep an eye on him. Later that night, my mom and I watched The Notebook and about half way through the movie, Dad said he was going to bed, went to my brother's room where he'd been sleeping, and shut the door. I said goodnight and fell asleep on my mom's lap with the movie still playing. When it was over, my mom woke me up to go to bed. I sat up and neither of us moved.

"What would we do?"

It was a question neither of us had addressed and I finally said out loud. What would we do if he went through with it? The threats weren't stopping and his desperation was growing. For the past couple of months his freedom had been slowly taken away from him. We removed his I.D., his drugs, his keys... anything that could aid in an attempt to leave and end his own life. But what if he really did it? What if he succeeded still somehow?

We had no answers to the ominous question before us. Rather we were left with more questions. I wonder now if God was preparing us for what was coming that night with our conversation. The conversation that brought mother and daughter even closer than before and strengthened us with a new determination to face whatever came our way in whatever way we could.

I went to bed with an awful sense of certainty that it would be a night unlike the rest. I barely slept. I think it was 3 AM when I finally dozed off for about an hour. I woke up suddenly and got up to go to the bathroom. The door to my brother's room was still closed. I went back to bed but didn't sleep again until about 5. It was 6:00 when my mom's voice echoed in my head. "He's gone!"

I practically fell out of bed and went to the open doorway of my brother's room. The bed was empty as I knew it would be. I turned and looked at my mom, still in her robe. She was shaken but not crying. My mind turned on auto-pilot and I went for my purse and keys ready to get in the car and go find him. Mom stopped me and it wasn't long before Dad called for the last time.

It was almost three weeks before we found out for certain that he was gone. That his pain was "all done."

Mark Macallister was father and friend, husband, son and brother. He was inspirational, unconventional, and brave. He was forgiving and generous, thoughtful and intelligent. He was dependable, strong, and loving. He was a "voice for the underdog"- a friend to the friendless. He was a hard worker, a wise teacher, and a kind listener. He was provider and protector. His character, despite persistent suffering, reflected Jesus.

*****

Daddy,

I love you. I miss you. I'm sorry I didn't understand your depression… that I let anger and fear build up in me. I wish, so badly, that I could tell you face to face. I wouldn't trade my time with you for anything. I'm still so happy that Jesus let me come live at your house. Thank you for loving me. Your best is good enough.

Bree

LEVI'S STORY

First, this is impossible: writing a single chapter in hopes of capturing an entire life. I tried to split it into "before" and "after," the way that tragedy divides all time, but I couldn't. Too much of what was "good" is the hardest to remember, and much of what was "bad" has been redeemed. Distinctions never moved past a darkened blur.

My grandfather used to follow his family around with an old, clunky VHS Panasonic camcorder. When he wasn't focused in on his feet, or my grandmother's behind, he was capturing our lives. Births, birthdays, holidays, t-ball games. It didn't matter much what was going on. If he had the camera on his shoulder, you'd see the red REC light shining toward whatever it was.

This year, I undertook a transfer project to see all of those home videos converted from analog to digital, figuring it would only be a matter of time before the film gave out, or melted in a box somewhere, and those memories would be gone forever. It's a huge project. I'm nowhere near done, and I'm sure there are a hundred more tapes where the first twenty came from.

When my mom and sister sit and reminisce about past days, I sometimes wonder if, at twenty-five years old, I'm already losing my memory. I have such a difficult time conjuring up specifics from my childhood. As I read through Bree's memories of our dad - whether painful or beautiful or both - I couldn't help but wonder if I'd be able to think of anything quite like what she'd surfaced, but I set my mind to the task.

163

I'm thankful for those moments that my grandfather captured, regardless of the family's regular pleas to put the camera down. I'm thankful for the time captured moments after my birth, when my dad held me in disbelief, terrified but certain that he was being introduced to a new kind of love. Or my sister's birth - terrified but certain he'd been given a miracle.

I love the video of my dad carrying me around the house on his shoulders, humming a tune that I can still hear - in his tone - as clear as day. I love the film's retelling of our time at the beach, together with my mom, where he carried around a boy young enough to justify not being able to remember it without the help, now. So, I have bits and pieces of memories, but they feel fragmented.

I know that we loved watching movies together. I know that the first R-rated movie I saw was Air Force One. I lay on the floor next to my dad when we lived on the Ranch in Southern California and saw Harrison Ford's plane torn down. My parents were usually sticklers about movies and I don't remember what made this one justifiable. On my fourth birthday, I told my dad that I wanted to go to Universal Studios, but I was afraid to tell him it was because I wanted to ride Jurassic Park; the movie was PG-13 and I wasn't allowed to watch it, so I told him I wanted to go because of the log ride, instead. I know that I always wanted to be the bad guy in movies. When we watched Star Wars for the first time together, it was under the stipulation that I would not start dressing up as Darth Vader. The next day I wore all black, and my dad gave me an hour's worth of chances to tell him the truth about why. I spent that hour lying between my teeth about how I was really Luke Skywalker wearing black during one of the scenes at the new Death Star in Return Of The Jedi.

He thought I was too fascinated with the dark side. It scared him.

I know why, now, but our parents did a good job of sheltering my sister and me from the fear that plagued Dad. One of the things that always dispelled any weight that I felt was his laughter. My dad had a laugh that could shake the room. I'd say it was proportionate to the despair that threatened to douse it, and in hindsight, I'm thankful for the times the light shone through his roar, like a battle won.

164

There are many things, now, that I appreciate so much more than I ever gave my dad credit for at the time. Perhaps, more than memories, I have respect. Appreciation.

I appreciate that he desired holiness. Even though he drowned in his own failure, he always longed that we would be a family who set our minds on things that were pure, honorable, lovely, true. He was careful to safeguard our hearts and minds. I think I have often recounted his pragmatics for doing so - cuss-word blockers for the television, music-restrictions if James Dobson didn't approve, etc - as separatistic. Perhaps that's unfair, and either way I can agree to disagree on some things, and simply thank God for my father's dedication to leading us in the wisdom and instruction of the Lord. He'd read the Bible to me. He'd read the stories of his favorite missionary journeys to me. During Christmas, we'd read Luke's gospel account of Jesus' birth, and he'd always redirect our attention to the true reason we had to celebrate.

I appreciate his willingness to have gone through the uncomfortable task of talking with me about sex. When I was twelve, we went on a real man's camping trip to a friend's cabin a few hours away from home. There was no electricity, so we chopped our wood for fire and light. We rode ATVs around the mountain. Dad talked me through all of the things that I have since seen fathers neglect in the lives of my friends who ended up learning about sexuality from the culture's distortion of it as either god or gross, rather than gift. He told me sex was awesome, and waiting for it would be even more awesome, so he encouraged me to pursue purity until the day singleness would give way to rejoicing in the wife of my youth. That conversation was invaluable, and I praise God that he didn't cower from it.

I appreciate his hard work and the ethic that surrounded it. Unfortunately, that virtue often caved to vice and ate him alive, but I know that when he stood before God, Satan had no ground to accuse him as having failed to provide for his wife and children. I take great joy in knowing that the devil is silenced there, since he spent so much of his time accusing my father otherwise.

He wanted to see Bree and me as children for as long as we

were able to remain so. Perhaps one of the saddest things I carry is that I don't feel like I ever took him up on that, but maybe that only sounds self-pitying. He used to look me in the eyes and tell me that he wanted me to have fun. Like him, it is one of the things I struggle with the most.

He loved people. I hear stories to this day from strangers and friends, alike, who I didn't even know knew my dad, about his deep compassion toward them in their times of despair.

There were good times - there were. T-ball. I remember how hilarious it was to my dad - the coach! - to see me chase my shadow as I ran the bases. My eyes fell on my own shadow as I scaled the diamond. I probably missed a lot of bases, but he'd always yell Safe! At home plate! even before I was able to play on a team - whether I was sliding into the living room carpet or impersonating a Dodger's triple hitter, or just falling over.

I loved skateboarding. Dad gave me my first skateboard. He took me to skate parks. He skated with me. He built a half-pipe for me in our backyard when we moved back to New Mexico. I've got pictures of us mixing concrete for the foundation while he wore a back brace to make it through the day.

I went to Asia with my dad when I was sixteen. Thailand, China, Burma, Laos. I hadn't realized until just now that it was almost the last time he visited those beautiful countries and their people for whom he gave his love and passion and life. Words will never describe the impact of what I experienced there, with him, as I encountered a people with a sacrificial zeal for Jesus unlike any I have ever met. Husbands whose wives had been raped for their Christianity. Widows whose husbands had been slaughtered for pastoring their village's people into the faith. I remember one story, distinctly: A woman's daughter had been found with one page of a Bible in her desk. Her teacher notified the authorities and, after asking her father to come to the schoolhouse, called for a school assembly. The children and faculty were lined up in a horseshoe-shape, with daughter and father in the middle, where they were shot and killed as an example to the school of the intolerable consequences of possessing Christian propaganda. I am confident that Jesus met them with the words, "Well done, good and faithful servants."

166

These were the people whom my dad loved and served and trained and pastored for over twenty-five years.

After he died, we received word from our foreign brothers that as far as they were concerned, his death was martyrdom beneath the tyranny of demonic oppression for the work that Jesus had done through him in Access-Restricted Asia. At the risk of over spiritualizing his suffering, I think Satan hated our family, and I think that even though I would have had it any other way, for all of the pain my father endured, it was ultimately grace that put a stop to it, and took him home.

He took me to Tiananmen Square. I skateboarded in the Forbidden City. We walked along the Great Wall of China together. We climbed the mount to a Buddhist holy place near the Golden Triangle where Laos, Thailand and Burma meet, and watched fires burn in the distance across country lines. We drove for hours into the Laotian forest to attend a hidden church service with forty-plus worshipers in a room the size of my kitchen.

I'm hesitant to say it, because I know that there has to have been a few more good times following that trip, but it's one of the last sweet memories that I can conjure. I suppose I couldn't ask for better. It wasn't long after returning that my dad started to get worse, and I started to grow distant.

The first time my dad disappeared, I was performing at a private event in Louisville, Kentucky. I flew in the day prior to the show to stay with a couple who I've since become close friends with, but at the time had never met before. When I answered the phone, I knew something was wrong.

"Levi, Dad's missing... he left a note..."

Rewind.

Maybe it's because my family was my normal, but I don't remember recognizing my dad's anxiety as peculiar growing up. I see it now. I remember him being temperamental. I remember his unceasing self-blame when something went wrong (or didn't). I remember that he assumed my friends and I didn't like him.

He often asked me, with prying suspicion, why I wanted to hang out at other people's houses more than our own. He'd ask me why I liked my friends' dads more than I liked him. Those assumptions always made me so angry, but my heartbreak, now, comes from seeing that he really wanted to know because he really believed it was true.

I remember my parents fighting. Phrases like "I'm the enemy" and, "It's always my fault" sounded like a skipping record whenever conversation got heated, elevated. Shouting and slammed doors. I never said anything. Maybe I was afraid. Maybe I thought it wasn't my place. Maybe I thought it was normal. My best attempt at pinpointing a time when I was bold enough to confront my parents, I was in high school. I don't remember the exact situation, but the essence of my statement was, "I will not be using you as role models for a healthy relationship." I don't know if my dad ever truly recovered from it. How could he? Who knew better than he that his marriage wasn't what he wanted it to be? Who knew better than he how it felt to have your son tell you that you were failing at the one thing you wanted to succeed at in hopes of redeeming your own youth? How claustrophobic had it felt to wonder how, if you can't even get a grip on yourself, you'd ever get a grip on your family?

Where that conversation lay in the midst of his final decline, I do not know. But it continually resurfaced, so I knew that even when his head cleared and my parents started to work toward health again, he never let it go. Besides, health was continually failing. It was a cloudy word.

I don't remember him having his back surgery. Where do these memories go? Is there some sort of psychological trauma that I have experienced to have completely erased such enormous moments? I only know that his condition rapidly worsened. Failed surgery. Unable to move. Immobilized on the living room floor. No more sleeping with mom. Perhaps all physical intimacy between them was impossible. It took three hours one day for my two best friends and me to drag my dad ten feet so that he could get back to his makeshift floor mat on the side of their bed in order to… not sleep.

No sleep.

He wept. I'd never seen, heard, felt weeping like my father's. My dad's.

I moved out when I was seventeen. I dropped out of college at eighteen and moved to Texas that summer. I started touring that year and was gone even more. I rarely went home. I don't have a reason. It wasn't malicious. But it wasn't thoughtful. I remember one day, perhaps the final summer that I saw my dad alive, going home, and repenting to him.

I'm so thankful for that day.

I had been at church wondering where God was. Wondering if He was. I went up for prayer after the service ended and my pastor started asking me questions that penetrated my heart. He always got to my heart. Somehow, the conversation turned to my neglect of my father and I drove home immediately following that service to apologize to my dad for never coming home, for never watching movies with him anymore. For leaving him alone.

He said I was forgiven.

I believed him.

Things were a little better after that. Sometime later, I told my parents that I wanted to marry Brandi, the girl whom I'd been dating for five years. My mom got excited. My dad's response was weird to me. I don't remember if he even gave me a yes or no, but I do remember him looking me in the eyes and, with sadness or joy or both, he told me that he was proud of me.

That fall I toured the West Coast by myself for two months. It was lonelier than I wanted it to be. I flew my girlfriend out to Seattle and proposed to her in our favorite coffee shop and then I continued the tour for two weeks longer after she'd gone back home. I'd tried hard to call my dad often on that tour and he acknowledged it. I'd spoken with my mom here and there and things seemed to be looking up. She was excited about our plans for the whole family to spend Thanksgiving in California shortly after I'd be home from tour...

The day I got back, she asked me to come home so that I could take my dad's guns out of the house. Something had happened to him overnight as he went from the man who held my sister's hair back while she was home sick from school, to the man whom my mother feared she'd find dead via shotgun in the spare room of her house. That night, when I left, weapons in hand, my dad started weeping, telling me that I was taking away his only hope for peace, and that after that brief moment of peaceful reprieve he dreamed about, he was going to go to hell, forever.

When I got the phone call saying he'd disappeared for the first time, I spent the whole night trying to get through to him. I spent the morning reading up on perseverance of the saints and memorizing Romans 8 in case he was still alive and I'd have the chance to talk him into sparing himself so that we could keep searching for answers. I performed for a private birthday party and put on a smile after we spoke - albeit briefly - and he promised that he'd not take his life... yet.

That night, he tried.

My sister met him at the hospital.

So began the whirlwind that was the final six weeks of his life.

At some point - and this is something that I've never told anyone - my dad called me to say goodbye. It didn't end up being the time that he finally took his life, but I could tell he was near the end. He told me that he hoped I would be able to remember the good times that we had together. There was a movie we had watched - I wish I could remember the name of it now - with a scene that made me laugh, to this day, harder than I have ever laughed before. My dad, too. We watched the scene over and over, probably 100 times, in our living room one night, after he had gotten pretty bad. We laughed so hard and so loud that we woke my mom and sister up and they came in and started laughing at and with us. We laughed for hours.

When my dad called me that day to tell me that he wanted me to be able to remember the good times after he was gone, he brought up that story, and he started laughing again. Right then, on the phone. Manic. He told me that he wanted me to remember that night. Him laughing. He said he hoped I could forgive the pain, and remember the laughter. Then he told me that he loved me, and said, "Goodbye, Son."

I assumed that was the end and that I'd truly just heard my dad's voice for the last time.

I never want to see that movie again.

My dad got out of the hospital after that attempt just before Christmas. I participated in the Christmas Eve service at our church that year and God gave him a bit of reprieve while he sat in attendance with my mom and sister. I was assigned a scripture reading from Zephaniah 3, and midway through, I found my dad's eyes in the audience and recited it straight to him. I read, *"The Lord has taken away the judgments against you; he has cleared away your enemies. The King of Israel, the Lord, is in your midst; you shall never again fear evil. On that day it shall be said in Jerusalem: Fear not, O Zion; let not your hands grow weak. The Lord your God is in your midst, a mighty one who will save; he will rejoice over you with gladness; he will quiet you by his love; he will exult over you with loud singing. I will gather those of you who mourn for the festival, so that you will no longer suffer reproach."*

After service, we went home. We ate together as a family. My father blessed the food and thanked Jesus for His kindness towards us. We watched The Polar Express.

That night felt like peace.

Indeed, it was the last night, but I can't help but take Zephaniah's words as a gift that Christmas. I knew they were for my father. I know they are for him. They were for us, too. The psalmist exclaims, "Precious in the sight of the Lord is the death of his faithful ones!" My father's is a God who turns death to life, mourning to cheer, anguish to rejoicing. He sings over His sons and daughters and lays waste the schemes of our enemy. He stills anxiety. He quiets all condemnations by His love. His roar, like my father's laughter, sings life.

The Apostle Paul says that nothing will be able to separate us from the love of God that is in Christ Jesus our Lord.

Most of the time, I believe Him, and the times that I fail to, do nothing to nullify the promise anyhow. It is grace that saves, grace that keeps, and grace that takes us home. I never knew Jesus loved me the way that He does until I got to experience Him as a Father in the place of my own. (I wish it could have happened any other way, but it didn't.) And that doesn't minimize the pain. It doesn't do away with the sin. It doesn't replace the loss. It doesn't always help when I find myself violently angry at the story that God has written.

But it is grace.

I don't think my dad was selfish to take his life. Frankly, I don't even think that he abandoned us. That outcome was inevitable, of course, but I think that if I were able to look at his decision through his lens, suicide was his last valiant attempt to love and provide for his family. And I weep as I write this, but I know with everything inside of me that he loved us until the end. His decisions were warped. His body and mind marred by the effects of sin and death. But not so far gone that I will vilify him. Not beyond forgiveness. Not beyond love.

Love does not fail. My father's strength and his heart failed, but love did not fail him. I longed to see my father healed on this side of death, and I did not. But that does not mean that he was not healed. Is not healed. He is.

My father's strength and his heart failed him for a life time, but Jesus Christ, the Son of the living, eternal Father God to whom my earthly daddy introduced me, is the strength of his heart, and his portion forever.

He rejoices over Mark Macallister with gladness.

*****

Dad, I am broken. Sometimes I feel like I'm breaking. These last few years have been hard. Life has been confusing and I wish that you were around so that I could ask you about it. Sometimes, I still come home from tour and think that I can call you. It's hard for me to think about Mom being alone, or Bree not having you to walk her down the aisle, or Brandi never having known who you actually were. Some days, I think I understand. . Some days, I think I hate you. It has occurred to me, as I have gotten older, and as my friends have become fathers, and as I have made friends with their fathers, that there could have come a time in our relationship where I could have seen you as more than an authority figure who regulated my life. I always saw parents as only parents, and maybe as people who had things figured out, but about a year after you died, I had a conversation with a father who had just given his son away in marriage. As he spoke, I looked into his eyes and saw myself. I saw fear and love and joy and he was sure and he was unsure and he was all of the paradoxical things that we are, and I wished in that moment that I could have gotten to know you as a friend. I finally realized that you were a child, and a young man, and a married man, and a dad - my dad who loved me - and you had to live this same life that I am living, and I wish that I would have realized that just a little bit sooner, so that we could have had that beer and smoked those pipes and had the conversations that you always longed to have with me. I'm sorry. God's joy over you gives me hope that He sings over me, too. I love you. I miss you. I can't wait to see you again.

Levi

Hi Jode :) I was going to write you a letter today, but I decided I'd write to you here thinking you might want to read this little Mexico journal in it's entirety sometime.

Ya Know, I've either forgotten or I've never known if my "Jode" rendition of your name is liked dis-liked or "max-mixed" by you. Well in any case, I'm afraid it's here to stay unless you direct me otherwise.

I'm sitting (½ lying) on a chaise lounge w/ three pads on it on a large patio overlooking the beautiful Pacific Ocean — which in part, occupies the hollow of God's Hand. I really wish you were here and that my back &/or your neck

maybe a little rubbing

would not prevent us from coaxing one another into a swim and body surfing together. And I'd be ok with you just reading a book beside me on a nearby chaise lounge.

I remember so well (in 3-D technicolor) sitting on the beach in Hawaii slightly reclined with you between my legs with head resting on my chest while we just talked — like two friends — about China and Jeff and life and loving Hawaii and ... what's next for you, for me ... for us!

I have so many fond memories since that Summer of '83. I am choosing to focus on them now Jody – and praying that God will not only give me back to you whole, but also for renewed vision and passion for us – Yes, first and foremost, in Him. But also "for us" in a way that doesn't exclude Him, but where friends and lovers are supernaturally natural. I guess it's all the same but through Spirit and not so much about "it requires hard "work" and formulas.

Late! Yvonne and I took a walk on the beach today – and gathered round, multi-colored stones for the Pirelos Star to be xeriscaped front yard. The stones look very much like river rock yet they are washed up in strong seas from the Ocean. It makes me realize that God can produce unexpected things from unexpected places. He makes ways, He produces and creates what He will outside the box of my understanding & even beyond my expectations...

Made in the USA
San Bernardino, CA
14 July 2018